FINISHING & REFINISHING

BY HARRY WICKS

HAMMERMARK STEP-AT-A-TIME BOOKS

PUBLISHER: HAMMERMARK ASSOCIATES
Floral Park, N.Y.

better building ideas for home workshoppers

Cover photography, Harry Wicks
All photographs by the author except those credited otherwise.

Book design, Alan Andresen
Technical art by Eugene Thompson (unless credited otherwise)

(G)

Library of Congress catalog number: 87-80429
ISBN 0-9618160-0-7
First printing 1987

PRINTED IN THE UNITED STATES OF AMERICA

For Justin--my Grandson and a brave little man

Acknowledgements

The author wishes to publicly thank all those who helped to make this book possible:
Ray Curletti; John Gaynor; Fred Hale; Al Sittner; Joe Provey; Peter Sweisgood; Gene
Thompson; Patricia Wicks; Jack Wicks; Jim Wicks.

FOREWORD

The first decision I had to make when I wrote my initial Finishing Book (for Grosset & Dunlap some 10 years ago) was to pin down just what audience that book would be for. In this re-do of that book which, happily, sold out, I have dropped some material in order to make room for more pertinent information of the late 1980's, such as Country Furniture Finishing. But, my goals have been the same. My experience as both editor and adult education woodworking teacher has me convinced that there are an awful lot of neophyte do-it-yourselfers out there hunting for good and reliable how-to information of all kinds. Additionally, in my direct contact with people--as a carpenter, builder, editor and teacher--I have come to the conclusion that most people are not looking to make a career out of one facet of do-it-yourself activities. Rather, they want good information presented in easy-to-read and follow style--with an index that gets them to what they need to know in a hurry.

To my mind, the two major mistakes that an author (and the book publisher) must avoid at all costs are--1. Don't create a book that's filled with fluff; 2. Don't write the book as though every reader plans to become the ultimate expert in that subject. In the first instance, a how-to book on any subject must provide its readers with easy to follow and reliable information. As an editor who has read thousands of manuscripts, I know all too well that the market is filled with DIY Pretenders. Avoid their books. The quickest way to find out a fake? Turn to the Index and look up several subjects that you have some reliable knowledge about--see how the author covered these areas. If you find information that's erroneous, or weakly understated, pass up the book.

Similiarly, it is in the book buyer's best interest to purchase a book that gives him a solid understanding of the basics. Many books mask their gross inadequacies in real expertise by filling page after page with hard-to-decipher and nonusable information. That is, with material that is of little or no use to the person who just wants a simple answer to a relatively simple question.

On these pages I have compiled information based upon conversations with, and questions from, customers in my woodworking shop, students in my woodworking class and readers of the publications I have worked on. By concentrating on the most often-asked questions, I have tried to supply readers with the answers--that

is, usable solutions--to those problems that seem most baffling to most of us. My intention here is to present the important how-to information in easy-to-follow "recipe" fashion, wherever that appproach makes the most sense---such as in how to apply varnish and tip it off. The result, HAMMERMARK'S Step-At-A-Time format, which , we hope , will help you solve your finishing and refinishing problems quickly and with the least aggravation.

And that is what you will find on these pages.

Harry Wicks

Floral Park, NY
February 1987

CONTENTS

1

GETTING STARTED IN FINISHING

You'll find a treasure of useful information in this book no matter where you rate your skills as a furniture finisher. Basically, this book is targeted at helping the beginner. Thus, it has been kept simple, with no unnecessary material, show-offy techniques, etc. The focus is on sensible, basic methods for the neophyte to follow so that frustration triggered by mistakes can be avoided.

But "old hands" at finishing will also find useful information in these pages because we have included professional tricks of the trade throughout. Knowing and utilizing these techniques are certain to make anyone's finishing or refinishing project easier, pleasanter and, most importantly, successful.

Make no mistake about it---for most of us, taking an old finish off or putting a new one on a piece of furniture does not fall into the "fun project" class. Despite inaccurate declarations stating the opposite in some magazines and how-to books, refinishing is, in fact, a lot of work. None of the projects that I've done were either "easy", "quick" or "fun" to do. The individuals who turn to refinishing as a hobby are rare indeed. The fact is that most refinishing projects are tackled because it is a job that *has to be done.* And since professional help in this area can get expensive, many of us end up doing at least part of our own refinishing. Thus, it makes a lot of sense to learn and use the right methods initially to save both time and frazzled nerves.

Happily, though, the job does get easier as you accumulate both experience and good tools. And when you finish a project the feeling is a rewarding one. There is a great deal of satisfaction as each project winds down to completion and those who view your labor of love--either the rejuvenated piece of furniture or the completed workshop project--do so with awe and respect.

Why refinish? Possibly the biggest reason these days is economics. Obviously, in most cases you'll spend far less money stripping, sanding, and refinishing an old piece than you would buying a new one of comparable value. This is especially true, of course, for antique--or near-antique--collectors.

Today there is also an increasing demand for furniture-in-the-raw, that is, unpainted furniture, which is often sold in knockdown, or kit, form. Because a lot of dollars can be saved, more and more people are buying such unfinished furniture, assembling it, if necessary, and finishing it themselves. Going this route saves the tedious sanding and stripping steps required to rejuvenate an old piece. But, though unpainted furniture is less expensive than buying furniture that is factory-finished, it is generally more expensive than rejuvenating flea market and garage sale finds.

A third group of active finishers/refinishers is composed of those who pursue the activity as a moneymaking hobby or sideline. Since skilled craftspeople come high these days--when you can find one--many sophisticated do-it-yourselfers are finding that refinishing, especially, can be a satisfying way to beef up their incomes while working at home. Such types generally have fully equipped workshops and first rate equipment to work with to make their finishing work a lot easier than it is for the average home do-it-yourselfer. Often, those who make money from this sideline divert a percentage of the income into maintenance of existing tools and purchase of new and better finishing equipment.

Another good and valid reason for refinishing--and, perhaps, the one that most will recognize--- is the desire to personally restore a valued piece of furniture that has been in the family for years. By now just about everyone has heard of at least one gem that's been found in a pile of junk either in attic or the garage. The occasional table shown on page 20 is an honest and perfect example of such a find. Located in the attic of their newly-purchased older home by a non do-it-yourself couple, "the monstrosity" was, happily, turned over to the author's wife--intact, with an 1873 newspaper still lining its only drawer.

The final group of finishers would be those active workshoppers who build most, if not all, of the furniture for their homes. This type (and the author admits to being one of the breed) would not even consider passing along a pece of furniture he's built for

Good-quality furniture such as this bedroom set by Thomasville Furniture Inc., will retain its good looks for years if it is properly cared for. See chapter 9. (Photo courtesy Thomasville Furniture Ind., Inc.)

Highly decorative veneers create dramatic beauty in this piece of dining room furniture. When veneers require refinishing, special care is needed, as can be learned in Chapter 8. (Photograph courtesy Thomasville Furniture Ind., Inc.)

someone else to put a finish on. This individual knows that it is more satisfying to learn the various finishing techniques and master them so he is able to do the piece entirely by himself--from lumberyard woodpile to in-home use.

That about covers the most basic reasons for wanting to learn more about finishing and refinishing. In this book, the emphasis is on a no-nonsense approach to the finishing basics. Exotic, far-out, or very special techniques will not be treated in detail in these pages. Instead, the focus is on the answers to those questions that I am asked most often, as professional cabinet-maker, teacher of an adult-education woodworking course, and resident woodworking expert for a national magazine.

BEFORE YOU START

Be advised that you owe it to yourself to take the time at the start to learn the very basics of working with the fundamental tools and materials. Halfway through a project is not the time to have to search for answers or solutions you should have had before you ever started. The same planning, or thinking ahead, also applies to how-to techniques.

In this book I have used only those materials and tools that I am personally familiar with. I know they will work for you because they have worked for me. All you have to do is follow the instructions in these pages and, when applicable, manufacturer's label instructions to be sure of success. All the products shown are available throughout the United States. For your convenience, should you have difficulty locating a particular product, all manufacturers of products discussed in this book are listed in the Appendix.

WHERE WILL YOU WORK?

If you already have a workshop you obviously have a head start. Your biggest problem will be to make certain that you keep the floor and the workbench free of slop created by stripping, and that your tools are similarly protected.

For health reasons, the room or area you decide to use should be well ventilated. If it lacks a pair of windows to provide cross-ventilation, you should give serious thought to installing an exhaust fan for removing odors and fumes.

The room should be heated for wintertime use because many of the materials must be used at temperatures above 50°F. The heat should not be from an open-flame source such as fireplace or stove, however. There is too much danger of an explosion caused by some of the flammable materials with which you will be working.

When weather permits, your backyard will probably be your open-air workshop. The ventilation is ideal, of course, and there is practically no breathing of fumes. And cleanup is easier. Out-of-doors you can also work with water-wash paint remover, using the garden hose to do the required washing off.

Always be aware of fire safety. No matter where you work, keep soiled rags in covered metal containers because of the high risk of spontaneous combustion. And, from the start, make it a rule that there be no smoking in your refinishing/finishing workshop once a project has started.

A final caution: never spray paints, lacquers, or varnish in a workshop basement where the oil burner is likely to start up during a work session. The spark in the burner's motor as it kicks on could trigger an explosion.

You'll also need a comfortable-to-work-at bench. This can be elaborate or kept simple to suit your own needs and preference. But there are several points to consider, no matter which way you go. First, the bench must be of a height that is comfortable for you. Though woodworking workbenches are usually 32" to 36" high, a finisher's workbench is generally more comfortable to work at if built lower, because of the nature of the work that takes place on it. Ideally, a finisher's bench is positioned at room center so that there is 360° access to the project without having to heft and move it about. The easiest setup is a pair of sawhorses, several lengths of 2x3 stock and a good-size piece of low-cost plywood. Here the table can be as high or as low as you want for a particular project; all you need do is put longer legs on the sawhorses, or shorten those already there.

If desired, you can build a large revolving table so that projects can be rotated while you stand in one spot. This is especially helpful when putting on finishes. To build such a table, use sturdy stock such as 2x4s for the legs, and make the fixed top of 3/4" plywood. The revolving top should also be of 3/4" plywood and mounted on sturdy Lazy Susan hardware. The table should be built so that the revolving work platform is about 18" to 20" from the floor so that large pieces of furniture will not be too high for you to work on them.

To assure professional-looking finishes, do equip your paint table with good overhead and side lighting. This allows you to continually inspect the workpiece from all angles as you apply the finish. By moving your head about to pick up light reflection, you will quickly spot any runs, sags, or "holidays" (a holiday is a spot that has been missed by paint or finish).

A photographer's floodlamp with a clamp-type handle makes a perfect finisher's lamp, and a fairly good-quality one can be purchased at reasonable cost. Most of the time you will leave it clamped in position, aimed at the workpiece. But the spring-type clamp arrangement lets you easily move the lamp to a different location or take it in hand for a moving hand-held inspection.

THINK OF YOUR ENVIRONMENT

Until fairly recently, unfortunately, almost nobody gave any thought as to what we were doing with our waste materials. And, that is sad: Many areas are now faced with acres of non-usable land, water sources are becoming contaminated, and so on. Make certain you dispose of all waste materials---including those used for stripping and finishing--according to the EPA and DEC rules and regulations for your area. If in doubt about them, check with your local municipality regarding this matter. In order to ensure adequate water and air for future generations, all of us must actively contribute to the efforts being made to reduce contamination. In fact, the time may not be far off when we will be held legally responsible, collectively and individually to do so.

SPRAY EQUIPMENT

These days more and more homeowners are buying spray equipment. Relatively high-quality, dependable spray equipment is no longer overexpensive and it is a worthwhile investment for those who plan to pursue finishing or refinishing as a serious hobby, in addition to painting their homes inside and out. Some makers offer models with roller attachments for the latter tasks.

When a spray finish is wanted on a small-scale shop project, those that come in the spray-type cans are highly desirable. (These paints and finishes do not contain the fluorocarbons felt by some to be damaging to the ozone layer of the atmosphere.)

The major argument against spray cans is that using them is an expensive way to paint or varnish. There is

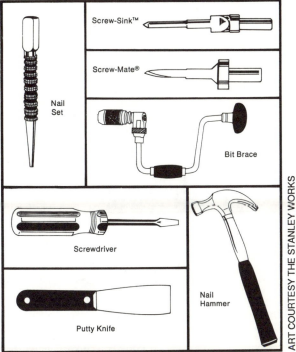

Basic tools you should consider buying:
Nailset--for setting nails below the surface without damaging the wood. Finishers are just as likely to use it for prying open paint cans.
Screw-Mate™--Available in a variety of sizes to suit the most-used wood screws. For use in an electric drill, this bit predrills holes for screw thread and shank, and makes a countersink for the head--all in one operation.
Screw-Sink™--Like the Screw Mate, it's intended for use in an electric drill. Does all that its counterpart does plus bores a counterbore so that the screwhead can be completely concealed beneath a dowel plug.
Bit brace and an assortment of bits--This is not a must if you own a portable electric drill and a good selection of various bits. Nowadays, the hand brace is used only on those jobs where meticulous craftsmanship is a must.
Screwdriver--Slotted shown but, at the very least, buy a medium size Phillips, too.
Putty knife--The refinishers "third hand".
Nail hammer--For most, a 13 oz. hammer with curved claw for easy nail pulling is the best choice.

no debate about that contention; thus, for large projects spray finishes in little cans are impractical. For a small one or two-can job, however, in my opinion they are indispensable. And, with a little practice it is possible to get very professional-looking results with paints and varnishes from spray cans.

A last word about your working conditions--and one that many may think so obvious that it doesn't require mentioning--be certain to wear your old clothing when you take on a refinishing or finishing project. Since these tasks are often messy ones--especially during the stripping, and staining and wiping steps--it makes a lot of sense to wear clothing that can be discarded, if necessary.

TOOLS YOU'LL NEED

Chances are you already own most of the basic tools

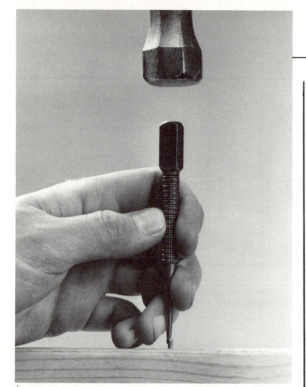

The correct way to use a nailset. The nail is driven until it is about 1/16" above the surface. The point of the nailset is then held in the dimple in the finishing nail's head and the nail is driven just below the surface. Always hold the nailset securely--or it is apt to skip off the nail and, strike the set with short smart blows.

constructed will increase your confidence in it and yourself as you use it. You should also know that brand-name manufacturers take a great many precautions to guard against defects in materials and workmanship. Such companies want you as a steady customer (marketing people call this brand loyalty) and they are well aware that the surest way of gaining your confidence is by delivering tools that don't fail.

As you start your tool collection, you are almost

TWO GOOD WORKBENCHES

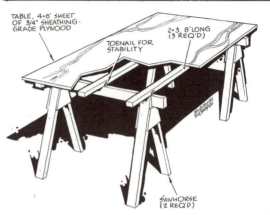

This workbench can be built for peanuts and disassembled for storage on the wall.

that are required during a typical refinishing or finishing operation. There are, however, some specialty tools that will make life a lot easier and let you do a better job in less time. You owe it to yourself to at least look over such equipment; don't automatically discount a particular tool's value, and the resulting possible advantages you can gain by owning it.

A word of advice: from the start, buy only quality tools. Many stores stock leader items, usually piled high on a table in an eye-catching location, that may look tempting. More often than not, such tools are priced low for one reason--they are of inferior quality. Shy away from such "buys". Seldom do these tools last longer than a job or two, and their mediocrity just might limit your ability and results. Furthermore, some of these tools are downright unsafe: i.e., a hammer head splits easily or flies off its handle after several swings. For your own peace of mind and for the sake of those whom may be standing nearby watching you work, ignore "cheapie" tools.

HAND TOOLS

Recommendations of the following tools are based upon the assumption that you have no tools whatsoever on hand: So, cross off any you may already own. At the least, you should know about all these tools, since each performs a particular task better than any other tool. Since you have made the decision to get into this finishing business, you should be aware from the start that proper use of good tools increases not only your degree of skill but your enjoyment of this chosen pursuit as well.

It is true that a tool that is carefully designed and well

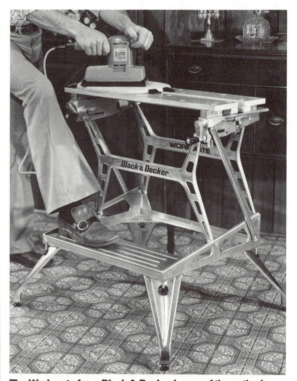

The Workmate from Black & Decker is one of the author's favorites. It serves as an excellent bench with two different work heights to choose from; it is also a super vise that grips and holds most of the household objects that you are likely to refinish.

Safety goggles should be considered a must for such tasks as furniture stripping and when working with power tools like the drill, sabre saw or sander. Respirator at left is a must to keep dust and fumes from your lungs; this version by 3M Co. has a replaceable filter.

certain to wonder in what order the various tools should be purchased. The list below is the preferential buying order for the majority of do-it-yourselfers. But the sequence is not etched in stone. You can jump the list to buy tools as they are needed. That, actually, is the name of the game. Since you are saving many dollars by doing-it-yourself, the idea is to channel some of those savings into labor and time-saving equipment. So, as a rule-of-thumb, begin by buying the most basic tools on the list--those that can be used for many or at least several tasks. Then as the need arises, you can add specialty tools, including many that aren't on this list at all.

PRIMARY TOOLS

13 oz. hammer with curved claw
12" combination square
Combination oilstone for
sharpening cutting irons,
Chisels
3/32" nailset
6' zigzag rule, or tape measure
Hand cutoff (crosscut) saw,
        24", 10 pt.
Hand ripsaw, 24", 5 pt.
Utility knife
6" block plane
Assorted *screwdrivers,* slotted and Phillips
Woodworker's vise
Coping saw, with extra blades

Chisels, 1/4", 1/2", 3/4",
        and 1" wide
Cabinet scrapers, one narrow,
        one wide
Assortment of *files and rasps,* flat, half-round and
        round; coarse, medium, and smooth.
Wire file card for cleaning
        file teeth
Countersink or bits with
        countersinks
7-oz. tackhammer
Putty knife

POWER TOOLS

3/8" portable electric drill . This drill does all that its smaller cousin, the 1/4 incher does, and more, because of greater chuck capacity. For versatility, spend a couple of bucks more and pick a model that boasts both reversing and variable speed. This allows the arm-saving advantage of being able to use the drill as a power screwdriver, if desired. If you will use your drill a lot, stay away from the 20 dollar versions because they are not built for continuous drilling. Drills in the $50 to $60. range should make most do-it-yourselfers happy. While you're looking at new drills, consider buying a cordless version. The higher-priced versions-- usually intended for professional use--are quite powerful and the batteries can be left in the charger when the tool is not in use.

Pad sander. Here you can choose from orbital or straight line models. The first is the type that often

Production sanding kit from 3M Company helps simplify sanding of wood, metal and plastics. This version is available in kit form containing five sheets of sandpaper and a comfortable-to-hold sanding block.

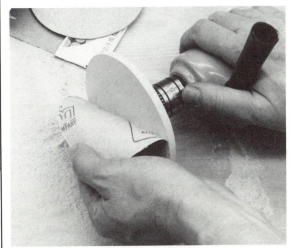

Sanding discs for use with an electric drill work fine when it is okay to sand in any direction. This stick-on pad version eliminates the familiar pad-holding washer and nut at center, thus increasing the amount of useful sanding area. 3M makes it.

Owning a small pad sander, they are also referred to referred to as finishing sander, is a must if you plan to do any amount of woodworking or refinishing. If you are critical about the way the sanded surface will look, make sure you select one with a high orbital speed. A slow-speed pad sander tends to leave little swirls in the finished surface. Also, to get the most sanding milage from your abrasive grits, make it your work habit to only buy top-quality sandpaper. Tip: You'll get even more from the sandpaper by cleaning it as you work. To do it, use either a brush with stiff-bristles or tap the paper against the workbench.

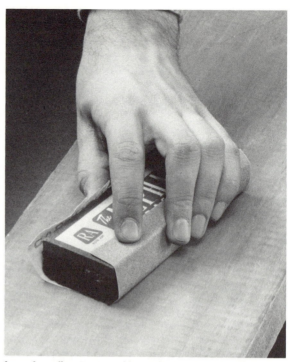

A good sanding stunt used by professionals that eliminates the fuss and bother of making a sanding block: simply wrap the paper around an ordinary, low-cost chalkboard eraser. Use the hard side to back up the paper when sanding bare wood: To smooth a surface after sealer coat, as here, flop the eraser and sand with the soft side down.

The belt sander is the workshop workhorse--and owning one is a must for all serious do-it-yourselfers. The model shown uses a 3 x 21" belt, one of the more common sizes available. When picking a belt sander keep in mind that the bigger the belt the heavier the tool. Too big can be arm-wearying over long sanding sessions. All belt sizes come in a variety of grits. Cloth belts are also manufactured so you can use the tool for straight-line polishing.

leaves little round swirls in the wood (if the speed is too slow). Straight-line sanders, as the name implies, have a forward/ backward motion that lets you sand with the grain. Some makers offer versions that work both ways by the flick of a switch. If you plan to do any amount of finishing, a pad sander is a must. For health reasons, pick one with a dust-collecting bag on it.

Belt sander. This is a dandy tool for heavyweight sanding jobs. A large selection of belts of varying grits is available to choose from in order to let you quickly and easily handle a wide range of sanding chores. Since a good-quality belt sander packs considerable punch, do practice on scrap first. The worst mistake to watch out for is "dishing out", which occurs if the sander is left spinning in one spot too long. Another is the rounding over at corners and edges caused by improper tool handling. Practice with this tool and you'll be glad that you did.

Sabre saw. This tool is a tremendous worksaver when you have to cut curves and scrolls. A sabre saw is especially helpful and useful for making interior holes because it can be used to make its own starting hole (called plunge cutting). Actually, this is a fun tool to work with once you have mastered it .

If you equip yourself with the abovementioned power tools you will find that you will eliminate about 75 percent of the hard work of refinishing in the finish removing and carpentry repair portions of the job.

PAINTING AND FINISHING EQUIPMENT

In addition to the carpenter's tools listed above, you will have to acquire some items intended especially for painting and finishing. These include:

Brushes. You'll need a pretty good variety of brushes for different materials and for the various job

Two Electric Drill Accessories You May Want To Buy: The small drum sander in the drill's chuck is great for getting into small curves, these are available in a number of diameters. The inexpensive horizontal drill stand frees both hands to hold the workpiece.

A vertical drill stand makes a portable drill a mini-drillpress. The device chucked in the drill here is a cup brush for removing rust and dirt buildup from metal surfaces.

An excellent tool for fast stock removal on irregular shapes such as scrolls, contours, spindles and the like, is the Grind-O-Flex brush sander. This version works great in both portable drill and drillpress.

Closeup photograph of the slashed strips shows how the sander works. Sandpaper rides the brushes and the slashed strips follow the contours of the work being sanded. When the sandpaper is worn, it is simply pulled out until new paper covers brushes; the worn portions are then snipped off.

applications. In general, use natural bristle brushes for alkyds, oil base, shellac and varnish; use nylon (or other manmade bristles) brushes for latex paints. Many manufacturers now offer all-purpose brushes and, for many, these are a sensible addition to a toolbox. However, my preference is to stick with the first choice above.

With one exception, always buy quality brushes. (More about that exception, later.) Clean a paintbrush thoroughly immediately after using it, first in appropriate solvent and then with a mild, soapy solution. Rinse with clear cool water.

NOTE: The only exception to the above brush-cleaning rule is with your shellac brush, which should be cleaned only with denatured alcohol after use.

When it dries the bristles will stiffen a bit, but they quickly soften for the next use by simply pressing the bristles against your palm.

To increase a brush's useful life, wrap its bristles in wax paper held by a rubber band after cleaning. Do not toss a brush into a drawer, hang it on the wall.

Artist's brushes. In several different sizes they are handy for tricky areas and for such tasks as striping and gold leafing. A pointed artist's brush is also useful for picking lint or dust particles from a newly-varnished surface.

Old, battered brushes. Don't throw out brushes that have "had it". They come in handy for applying paint and varnish removers. Get this one last use from such brushes, *then* throw them out.

Sandpaper, steel wool. You will use a considerable amount of both so, for convenience,

Refills for both size wheels offered by Merit Abrasive are available. The slashed-strip type (refill) is in the foreground, solid-strip type is on the large wheel atop the block of wood. A steel wire wheel, for tasks on metal, is against the block.

This-and-that make good tools too. Household items that become finisher's tools include coarse twine for use in grooves on legs, burlap, old toothbrush, toothpicks, and orange sticks. All are useful on stubborn, hard-to-clean-out areas.

keep a good supply on hand. In sandpapers, keep a stock of grits from coarse through very fine. For steel wool chores pick up a half-sleeve of each texture from 1/0 through 4/0 grades (the latter being the finest texture).

Tools that cost almost nothing. Save old twine, orange sticks, toothbrushes--anything that might serve to remove paint or varnish from nuisance areas such as in crevices and turnings.

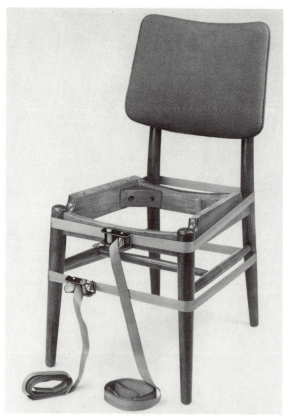

Band, or web, clamps are used to encircle round and irregular shapes—tables, chairs, etc. And, they are surprisingly inexpensive. To use a band clamp, the band is placed around the work and drawn snug by hand. Final pressure is applied with a small wrench that comes with the clamp. A self-locking cam gives positive hold, instant release. (Photo courtesy The Adjustable Clamp Co.)

Finishing materials. Paints, shellac, varnish, solvents, etc. You should acquire these as the need arises. Contrary to popular opinion, do not buy your finishes in large-volume containers unless you are certain you will use the materials within a reasonable amount of time. Like many commodities, finishing materials have a shelf life, after which they should be thrown out. Remember that an overage finishing product is the one that will likely never dry, but always remain tacky. When this happens you are back at square one--stripping.

I mark the purchase date on paint can bottom with a permanent felt marker. In general I hold onto shellac for about 6 months, varnishes oil and latex paints for 12 months. After those periods of time expire I dispose of the sealed containers according to the regulations at our local town dump.

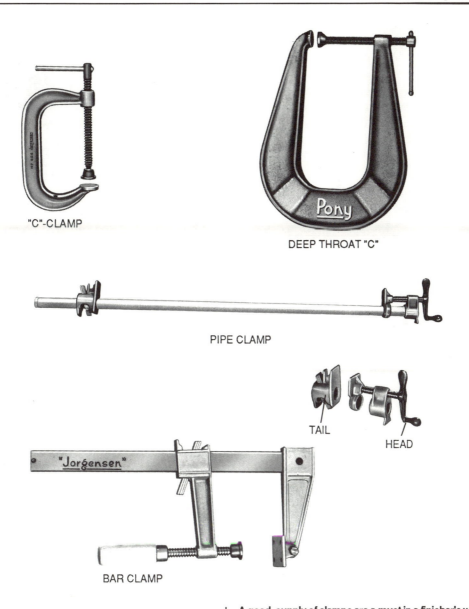

"C"-CLAMP

DEEP THROAT "C"

PIPE CLAMP

TAIL

HEAD

BAR CLAMP

A good supply of clamps are a must in a finisher's workshop. Here's a rundown on the types that you are most likely to use:

"C"-clamp: regular throat, for general use.

"C"-clamp, deep throat: gives extra reach . I.E., for clamping interior of two hard-to-reach surfaces to be joined. For example, to apply pressure to the field on a countertop.

Steel bar clamp: Several versions of bar clamps are available, and just about all of them are great. These provide super clamping power over long reaches. Size of clamp is determined by length of bar. Thus, for example, if you want to clamp something that's 31" wide, you would buy 36" clamps.

Pipe clamps: Used for the same tasks that bar clamps are used for but, are far cheaper because you purchase the head and foot only and use 3/4" dia. black pipe as the bar. With these you can keep a variety of lengths of black pipe on hand in your shop and use the same head and foot for just about all your clamping jobs, no matter the reach needed. These do the job but, author prefers working with bar clamps and has stocked his shop with a variety of different-length bar clamps.

(Drawings courtesy The Adjustable Clamp Co.)

Steel spindle handscrews have jaws of hard maple thus, they are less apt to yield under pressure. Screws can be used singly, in pairs, or in combination with each (or other clamps) to achieve good clamping action, as illustrated here. (Photo courtesy The Adjustable Clamp Co.)

Spring-type clamps work fine on jobs where parts won't slip or slide. Add at least one pair of these to your toolboard.

2
STOCKING MATERIALS...
WITHOUT
OVERDOING IT

In the best of worlds, like your toolbox, your materials closet should be stocked so that once you start a project you can work without interruption. This doesn't mean that your workshop has to look like a paint store, but it does suggest giving sufficient thought to your needs for the upcoming job so that you can purchase materials to suit---without either over or underbuying. Almost nothing is peskier than having to stop in the middle of a stripping chore because you have run out of remover. Because of the task you're working on, chances are you will have to wash up and change clothes before you run to the paint store--then change back to work clothes upon your return.

Basically, finishing furniture breaks down into five tasks:

- Sanding and dusting off

- Staining

- Sealing

- Finishing or painting

- Waxing--an optional step

If you are refinishing an old piece add these three steps upfront:

- Stripping the old finish

- Bleaching--not always needed

- Carpentry repairs--if required

PAINT AND
VARNISH STRIPPERS

Until commercial paint removers came on the scene, unwanted finishes were generally removed using either broken pieces of glass, metal scrapers and blow torches, or a combination of these. Though these tools did eventually get the finish off, they were as likely as not to remove parts of the furniture as well. The incidence of damage caused by such tools was high, and to say that these finish removal procedures was tedious borders on understatement.

Early use of caustic solutions containing lye, trisodium phosphate, soda ash, or potash were effective in removing surface coatings but these also did a great deal of damage to the piece and its wood. Injury to the user's hands, clothing and the surrounding work area was not uncommon either.

By contrast, today we can walk into almost any paint or hardware store and purchase a pint, quart, or gallon of liquid or paste remover that will soften and lift just about any finish, without requiring a Herculean effort by the user. Strippers/removers are available in a great variety of brand names.

Commercial removers work as solvents for mediums (linseed oil and resins) in which shellac, varnish and most paints are suspended. The beauty of most commercial paint removers is that you are able to remove all finishes on a piece with the one product. Occasionally, you will come across a substance that does not react to a commercial paint remover (the milk paints used a century or more ago are one good example of this). Often called "stubborn paint", this problem is usually found on antique pieces under another finish, and is only discovered after a paint remover has stripped away the top finish. More about this in Chapter 3.

Choosing which paint remover to use from the three available types--paste, thin-liquid and thick-liquid--is generally a confusing experience for beginning refinishers. Be advised that most professionals prefer to work with the faster-acting thin-liquid type. But recognize that the remover's fast action also steps up the pace at which you must work--and that's something that most beginners are not likely to appreciate. Thick-liquid remover has a syruplike consistency; as a result, it is slower drying and gives a longer working time. The paste removers are pretty messy to work with but are a must when removing a finish from vertical or near-vertical surfaces.

Along with a paint remover you will need a can for holding the remover while you work--a 2-lb. coffee can is perfect because it will accommodate most brushes. You'll also need an old paintbrush (remember our suggestion in Chapter 1 to save old, worn brushes for just one more use), scrapers, putty knife--preferably a dull one with rounded corners, rags, burlap, twine and solvent. Orange sticks and toothpicks are useful for cleaning out carvings, crevices, etc.

PAINT REFINISHERS-- THE NEW BREED

Until recently, redoing an old piece of furniture to remove yellowed varnish, lacquer or the like automatically meant that you had to go whole-hog with paint strippers. But that is no longer the case. In those instances where you simply want to lighten the finish for a "Country Look" for example, you can do it in a single work session with a refinisher.

Several manufacturers now market a refinishing product called simply, Refinisher. It is, basically, a mixture of acetone and toluene which, when applied to many finishes, tends to break down and redistribute the finish, rather than remove it entirely. When this mixture is correctly used, it quickly, and with very little effort on the user's part, alters the old finish to an antique-like look. Instead of the wood looking bleached or white, as it does with paint remover, some stain and wood color, or patina (due to the aging process) remain. You do not have to apply a coat of stain to restore grain appearance.

The author has worked with Refinishers made by Formby, Minwax and UGL and has found all three do the job intended.

BLEACHES

Bleaching is called for only when it is necessary to lighten the color of the wood or if it is necessary to remove stains. In general, it is best to use the commercial two-part bleaches. Some must be intermixed, while others are applied in successive steps. No matter which type you buy, be advised that all of them contain strong chemicals so make certain you wear both rubber gloves and safety goggles when using the stuff. It's also smart to wear either a work apron or old clothing because the bleaches will attack most fabrics. Make certain you read and follow label directions.

Bleaches can be applied with either brush or sponge and should be allowed to dry on the surface until the desired effect is reached. The instructions on the package will tell you whether or not a rinsing is required to stop the bleaching action. After bleaching and rinsing, let the piece dry thoroughly, at least 24 hours. Then sand lightly with a very fine sandpaper taking care that the sandpaper does not penetrate any deeper than the bleach did.

PRO TIP *When sanding wood during a refinishing project, keep in mind that the dust created will contain dried particles from the previously-applied stripper or bleach. For this reason, always wear a respirator when*

sanding a refinishing/finishing project, so you don't inhale those particles. Work outdoors if possible; if not, make sure your shop is well ventilated.

In some cases ordinary laundry bleach (such as Clorox) can be used to bleach wood. This is applied and handled in much the same manner as the commercial bleaches, with the exception that vinegar is used as neutralizer or rinsing agent. Laundry bleach won't handle the tougher jobs.

TOOLS AND MATERIALS FOR MINOR REPAIRS

After stripping a piece of furniture, and during and after the sanding operation, take the time to carefully check the piece for minor defects. Cracks, holes and dents are all repairable by the do-it-yourselfer who has a fair share of common sense. To make the repairs you'll need such items as:

GLUES

Regluing is the very essence of most furniture repair. Glue applied properly and left to dry under pressure (e.g., clamped) is probably the surest way there is to craftsmanlike and long-lasting repairs. Today the myriad of glues available is confusing when you walk into a hardware store to pick an adhesive for a project. And, more likely than not, the salesperson will be of little or no help to you because many of them rarely use the products they sell. For this reason, do take the time to become familiar with the various glues---what each does, etc.

Be advised that, in general, for furniture repair the waterproof resin glues are best. This is the type that usually comes in two parts--one containing the liquified resin while the other part is the powder catalyst that triggers the gripping properties of the resin. There are also available non-waterproof resins--powders to which you simply add water.

Perhaps the most popular glue these days is the familiar white glue. This is a plastic, quick-drying type, generally a white vinyl, which is transparent when it dries. This is an excellent glue for parts that will not be subjected to sustained pressure when in use. It is not waterproof.

A more recent entry into the DIY glue scene is the one that looks like a yellow version of white glue. Called Carpenter's Glue, this is an aliphatic-resin glue that grabs faster (than white glue) on initial contact, yet it allows the parts to be repositioned for clamping. It's fast drying and most brands offered have a high resistance to heat. Work can proceed after only about one hour of clamping.

Epoxy glues are on the expensive side but they do give strong and lasting results when properly used. The big advantage with an epoxy is when it is used to join porous to nonporous surfaces, such as a piece of metal to a wooden drawer front. Epoxy glues are also useful on many other kinds of materials as you will learn by reading the manufacturer's literature and labels.

Filling Holes

You will need on hand a supply of wood fillers for patching minor scratches and other surface defects. These are sold in various wood colors for matching as close as possible to woodtones. Apply filler with a putty knife forcing it into the crack and immediately scrape off any excess. The idea here is to fill the scratch only--not to coat the surrounding area. When dry, thoroughly sand the filled area.

Another way to fill minor defects is to wait until after the entire piece has been refinished. Holes can then be filled using wax putty sticks, the kind that looks like crayons. These are sold in lumberyards and home centers for use on prefinished wall paneling and are perfect for many furniture scratches. Briskly rub the stick back-and-forth across the scratch; the heat generated by friction causes the waxy substance to melt somewhat and fill the hole. Then, using a clean, soft cloth, wipe off all excess. You should know that you can buy sticks of varying colors and mix and match them to create a perfect blend with an offbeat, or unusual, color tone.

Sometimes it's better to color a scratch rather than fill it. This is generally true when the scratch is a clean and rather small one. Instead of having to sand the surrounding finished area to a feathered edge for the conventional patching methods, you can often make the scratch relatively invisible by tinting it with an ordinary household item such as black coffee, tea, shoe polish or iodine.

Other Items You Should Keep On Hand

Some repairs will call for hardware. For example, a corner brace or angle iron might be needed to beef up or close a corner tightly. Flat fasteners, called mending plates, are available in a number of shapes and sizes for use over cracks in flat areas. If you plan to refinish a number of old pieces requiring minor repairs, you are well advised to lay in a modest supply of various plates and braces. And, start building a supply of screws for use with this hardware. Besides the convenience of having the hardware on hand when you need it, be aware that it is a lot less costly to buy such hardware in volume; that is, in loose bulk at your hardware store--than it is by the blister package containing one or two pieces.

Large holes or gouges in bare wood can be filled with one of the wood doughs or with a plastic filler of the type that is available at hardware and paint stores. The first type is usually mixed with water; it is generally the better choice for huge holes. The second type comes ready to use--but be aware that it hardens rapidly when exposed to air. Don't automatically toss it out, however, when it hardens. Often it can be resoftened by pouring-in some lacquer thinner and recapping the can. Remember that this type of filler absolutely *does not* take stain--no matter what the manufacturers claim. To be safe, test on scrap before using on a treasured piece. The bottom line? Use a plastic wood filler when the finish will be a paint.

This and That From Your Shop Scrap Box

Your scrap box, more often than not, is filled with any number of items that do, in fact, have considerable project value. That's why so many shop buffs (including the author) seem to continually wind up with boxes and boxes of "goodies" and racks filled with small pieces of lumber--too valuable to throw out.

It makes sense, for example, to keep such items as various-size finishing and corrugated nails, Scotch fasteners, and the like, where you can get to them easily should the mood to refinish something strike you at an unusual hour or on a weekend.

ABRASIVES

Coated abrasives, commonly called sandapers, are available with either paper or cloth backing. The first comes in four weights and the second in two. The two other backings solid-fiber and fiber combination--are for specialty sandpapers and are not generally available to the consumer. The sandpaper backings are coated with various types of minerals, and each kind is for a specific use.

Basically, there are five types of abrasives that you should know about so you can make an intelligent choice (that is, make a product selection that will save you the most work) when picking an abrasive or two for a particular project:

• *Silicon carbide* This is considered to be the sharpest and hardest man-made material known. Blue-black in color, it comes coated on both cloth and paper backings. It is particularly effective for sanding low-tensile metals, plastics, copper, aluminum, etc. When used in combination with water it is excellent for sanding primed surfaces and for featheredging between coats, as is often necessary when painting metals. It is fine for soft woods, paint and varnish finishes.

• *Aluminum oxide* Like silicon carbide, this is a product of the electric furnace. Considered to be the toughest and most durable abrasive grain made today, it is generally brownish in appearance. Coated on both cloth and paper backings, it is good for all types of wood and metal.

• *Flint* A natural mineral abrasive, usually milky white in color. Generally coated on a paper backing, it provides a smooth finish on wood. Don't use it on metal. This is the cheapest sandpaper but, generally breaks the fastest on a pad sander--usually up around the front clamp.

• *Emery* This is also a natural abrasive, frequently dark gray or black on a blue cloth backing. Excellent for removing rust and corrosion from metals and as a polishing abrasive.

PRO TIP *Emery cloth is a great abrasive tool for smoothing a project while it's still mounted on the wood lathe. Simply tear the desired grit into narrow strips and use the strips shoeshine fashion to sand a* spindle while it spins at high speed in the lathe. The emery cloth is tough and does not break easily, despite the heat generated by the friction of being held against a fast-spinning block of wood. Try it.

•*Garnet abrasives* These are easily spotted because of their orange color. Available in both cloth and paper backings, garnet paper is used for sanding all types of wood.

Coated abrasive products are sold in various degrees of grain or mineral sizes. One method is to label the sandpaper *fine, medium* or *coarse.* But most sandpapers are graded by number--the lower the number, the coarser the coating. Grades from 12 to 600 are commonly available at paint and hardware stores. Though there are more than 20-grit sizes available, you will generally work with those grits numbered from 60 to 280. The coarser grits (that is, up to about 120) get you started on bare wood while the finer ones come into play when sanding between finishing coats.

PRO TIP *Don't automatically reach for an 80-grit or coarser sandpaper when getting ready to start finishing a wood project you just completed. In most cases, 80-grit or coarser will make the surface rougher than before you ever touched it. The finished (dressed) lumber that you get from the lumberyard is so smooth these days that the roughest grit that should touch it is 100. On almost every project, especially when working in pine, the author does the first bare-wood sanding with 100-grit and the second and final bare-wood sanding with 120 grit.*

Before. This occasional table, a gift to the author's wife, is in obvious need of some minor repairs and refinishing.

Steel Wool

This is used after sanding when a particularly smooth finish is desirable. Like sandpaper, steel wool comes in various grades of coarseness beginning with a very coarse No. 3 and going to very fine No. 4/0. Most professionals agree that Grade No. 1 is the coarsest steel wool that can safely be used on furniture. Use that grade for the first rubbing on turnings, crevices and the like. As the work progresses, switch to a finer grade of steel wool.

Be aware that steel wool disintegrates as it is used. Thus, make certain you take care to protect skin, eyes and lungs. In fact, you are well advised to wear both gloves and safety goggles when using steel wool. And, when you use steel wool to polish a spinning piece in the lathe, wear a mouth respirator to keep the particles from being breathed in.

PRO TIP *Though steel wool is an abrasive, it is not intended to replace sandpaper. Actually, steel wool is used to polish a piece, not smooth it. It is a superior tool when used for waxing a piece: see our suggested method in Chapter 5.*

After. Here's how project was handled 1,2,3: 1, Piece was stripped to the bare wood . 2, Minor carpentry repairs were made, i.e.; the crack in its top was closed using glue and clamps and the ill-fitting, thin plywood shelf above the drawer was replaced with 3/4" thick material. 3, All parts were sanded smooth. Some interesting findings after the old finish was removed—A, There are three woods in this table—maple, oak and pine. B, One leg—the front left one—is probably from an earlier patch/repair job. Though it comes close, it does not perfectly match the other three legs. C, What appeared to be a wooden knob on the drawer turned out to be solid brass when cleaned off.

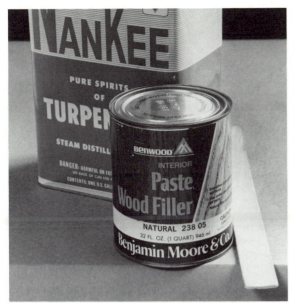

Paste wood filler comes in a can like this--it doesn't look anything like the cans that wood patches and fillers come in. Paste wood filler is thinned to consistency of heavy cream, using turps--see chapter 4.

PASTE WOOD FILLERS

These should not be confused with the synthetic wood fillers that are intended for use when patching indents and scratches in bare wood. Paste wood fillers are used to fill the open grains that are present in certain hardwoods. Some hardwoods--but not all of them--have large, obvious pores which must be filled to assure a smooth final finish.

PRO TIP *Some professional finishers prefer to not fill the pores under certain conditions. For example, if you build an oak piece from the Victorian period (such as the Icebox offered by Hammermark Associates) you*

may not want to fill the pores. In these cases you simply pass-up the paste wood filler step.

When to Apply Wood Fillers

If the piece you are finishing is to be painted, the paste wood filler is used prior to any painting, before the primer coat. On the other hand, if the furniture will be stained, the paste filler follows the stain--but precedes the application of the clear finish.

Though paste fillers are available in colors to match the various stains on the market, the author prefers to work with the (neutral) filler that most paint stores stock. This filler can be colored or tinted to match by adding some of the stain that was used on the piece, alone or in conjunction with pigments in a tube.

As the name implies, paste filler is sold in paste form; thus, it must be thinned for use. To do it, read and follow the manufacturer's instructions for thinning. Generally, thinning should be done with either turpentine, benzine or naphtha.

PRO TIP *The author does not wish to pick on salesclerks but, personal experience has proven time and again, that most sales-clerks are not familiar with paste wood fillers, thus, will try to push a plastic wood filler when you ask for Paste Wood Filler. If you have never used the stuff, one way to make sure that you get the right product is to order it by brand name. A national brand name that the writer is familiar with and uses is, Benwood Paste Wood Filler manufactured by the Benjamin Moore Company.*

That pretty much covers those materials that you are most likely to need and use as a beginning finisher. The other important materials, such as stains, varnishes, etc., are discussed as we get to the various techniques recommended. You can be sure that there are other materials you will learn about as your do-it-yourself skills increase. But now that you are armed with the right basic tools and materials knowledge, in the next chapter we will get into the nitty-gritty of finishing and refinishing.

3

REFINISHING-- WHERE TO START

Now that you have bought that flea-market treasure or the "whatsit" you could not resist at a garage sale, what are you going to do with it? Can you use it as is? Will a thorough cleaning make it usable? Or, more likely, will you have to strip it down to the bare wood so you can apply a finish that will blend beautifully with the decor in the room in which it will be used? Chances are, the last course is the one you will take.

Back in your workshop the only thing you can do is start logically. If you want to save the existing finish, step one is to determine exactly what it is so you will know exactly which materials to use in the ensuing steps. If, on the other hand, you plan to either strip the piece yourself, or take it to a professional for a finish-removing bath, it does not matter what finish is on it.

IDENTIFYING THE FINISH

When it comes to dirt-encrusted aged furniture, it is almost impossible to tell at a glance just what the furniture might be made of or finished with. But, happily, there are some things you can do to help you determine just what you may have hauled home. In broadest terms, any piece of furniture you may decide to refinish is most likely coated with one of the finishes listed below (or, even with a combination of them). Here's how to figure out what you must deal with.

Lacquer

This finish is used mostly by professional finishers and in furniture factories. Lacquer came into its own during the 1920's; it was quickly adopted as a favorite by furniture manufacturers for several reasons. It is sprayable, fast-drying and quite durable; these characteristics make lacquer ideally suited to production purposes. But, be aware that lacquer is one of those finishes that requires protection from heat, cold and moisture. It is not as tough as a varnish.

To determine whether or not a piece has a lacquer finish, in an inconspicuous spot clean away all dirt with soap and water. Then moisten a clean cloth with lacquer thinner (acetone, nail polish remover) and rub that spot continuously for several minutes. If the finish is lacquer, it will soften in about five minutes. Be advised that there are tinted lacquers; thus, a painted chair could actually have a lacquer finish. Many of today's factory-finished kitchen cabinets, for example, come with a colored lacquer finish.

Shellac

This finish is made from the excretion of the lac bug, and until the middle of the nineteenth century, practically all furniture was finished with shellac. Testing to find out whether or not a finish is shellac is basically the same as that for lacquer. The only difference is that the solvent used to moisten the cloth here is denatured alcohol.

Shellac-lacquer

Though it is possible, it is not very probable that you will come across a piece of furniture with this finish on it. Some early furniture makers in the United States created a lacquer-shellac by combining the two materials. It can be spotted on an old piece when an area that has been rubbed with alcohol becomes gooey and soft but does not run. Lacquer thinner also softens this finish in the same manner. In effect, either solvent merely softens its mating finish.

Varnish

If rubbing with denatured alcohol or lacquer thinner does not soften the finish, it is a pretty safe bet that you're dealing with varnish. Because varnish is slow-drying, most large furniture manufacturers shun it. On the other hand, because of its toughness and durability, many small shops and custom furniture builders prefer working with varnish. Without a doubt, a water-resistant varnish is the best choice for a furniture finish for the majority of do-it-yourselfers.

Varnish has the characteristic--unlike shellac or lacquer--of remaining pliable after years of exposure. It is possible to draw a fingernail or toothpick across the surface to create a slight indentation in the finish.

Refinishing--Where to Start

Type of Wood	Grain	Filler Required
Hardwoods		
Ash	Open	Yes
Birch	Close	No
Cherry	Close	No
Chestnut	Open	Yes
Mahogany	Open	Yes
Maple	Close	No
Oak	Open	Yes
Poplar	Close	No
Walnut	Open	Yes
Softwoods		
Basswood	Close	No
Fir	Close	No
Pine	Close	No

The woods that you are most likely to work with in your woodworking projects. Notice that only the close-grained hardwoods require the use of a paste wood filler to ensure a smooth finish. Failure to use a paste filler on an open-grained wood increases the liklihood of small (pin) holes being visible in the finished coat.

Generally, this is the only test you need conduct to determine whether the piece is varnish-coated.

Oil and wax

If the piece is natural looking, that is, not coated with paint or stain, chances are that it was originally finished with either boiled linseed oil or a wax. Both of these finishes are in favor these days because they suit two very popular home furnishing styles--American Country and Scandinavian Contemporary. Additionally, these finishes are easy to work with; application is fast, and the resulting look is a pleasant one, especially when the furniture has a handsome woodgrain. No matter which of these finishes is on your furniture, both when the furniture has a handsome woodgrain. No matter whlch of these finishes is on your furniture, both types must be removed before any other finish can be applied.

To remove linseed oil, use turpentine and 3/0 steel wool. Don't rub too hard with the steel wool or you will polish the wood thus making it almost impossible to apply stain evenly. Limit your choice of stain and finish to the oil-based types.

A wax finish can present other problems. Very often, wax penetrates so deeply into the wood that it is impossible to safely apply any other finish--ever. As far as I know, currently there is no finish available that adheres well to a waxed surface. You can try cleaning the surface in a manner similar to the method suggested for boiled linseed oil, above. Again, stick with an oil stain and varnish for the new finish.

Other finishes

Penetrating resins are used by some--particularly on pine--in order to create a hard surface. Resins, which soak into the surface and harden the wood fibers, come water-clear. Thus, if a certain color or tone is desired, the wood can be treated with a stain before they're applied.

Resins cannot be removed using standard stripping procedures. Generally, sanding is the only way to get a penetrating resin off a piece. But you should be aware that, since resins penetrate quite deeply, you will have to remove a considerable amount of wood by sanding.

The synthetic varnishes on the market today create problems for refinishers. Such chemicals as polyurethane, phenolic, etc., are extra-tough and offer a high degree of resistance to almost all chemicals. In fact, some will even resist paint removers.

You won't have any trouble identifying a painted piece, of course; all paints can be removed with conventional methods and commercial removers..

REJUVENATING FURNITURE WITHOUT REFINISHING

Frequently, a dirt-covered piece of furniture will require nothing more than a good, careful cleaning to be ready for use. It doesn't happen often but, there's always the possibility that a chair or a chest you've bought will be usable immediately after a thorough washing. Unless you're a furniture expert, be realistic and chalk up such a happy find to pure luck, and accept the fact that you won't often enjoy such good fortune.

Refinishers

We referred to refinishers in Chapter two. This is a neat product to use on any piece that requires minimal work. The beauty of refinisher is that it is very easy to work with and takes little time. Since the fumes can be overpowering for many of us, make sure you use it only in a well-ventilated room or outdoors. Basically, the steps for using refinisher are shown in the captioned photographs but, you should take the time to carefully read the use- instructions on the label of the can that you buy, before you start.

Cleaning Old Furniture-- Where to Start

If the furniture has had reasonably good care, any dirt buildup will generally be in the wax that was applied to protect the finish. So, logically, the smartest way is to start by cleaning off the old wax. After this is done, you will be able to inspect the piece to determine what your next step should be. To remove wax , use either turpentine (turps) or a commercial wax remover, and clean cloths.

Start by removing all hardware from the piece, setting it aside for its own separate cleaning session. Then apply generous amounts of the solvent to the areas to be cleaned. Wipe with a circular motion and permit the solvent to remain on the surface for at least 10 minutes. Next, wipe off using a clean, solvent-dampened cloth. During the rubbing off action constantly rearrange your cloth work to ensure keeping clean rag in contact with the surface. Keep repeating this process until a clean cloth no longer picks up any dirt and/or wax.

REFINISHERS--A HANDSOME FINISH IN JIG TIME

If your antique find is in sound structural shape and all you'd like to do, basically, is lighten its finish, it is possible that you can get the exact results you want by using Refinisher. Here are the proper steps for working successfully with this new material. *Caution:* The product contains acetone and toluene and should be used only in a well ventilated area.

2. Pour refinisher into the clean container and saturate a 000 steel wool pad; then, squeeze out excess. Periodically repeat this dipping procedure as refinishing goes on.

Before: A small oak turning was selected for use as a sample to do these steps and photographs for the book. Oak is too dark to suit today's tastes; dark finish hides a handsome grain.

3. Rub the steel wool with the grain whenever possible. On this piece some of the finish was deeply embedded in the oak's pores. These areas required some extra rubbing.

4. After rubbing-down the entire piece, repeat the rubbing step using a new, clean steel wool pad and a clean (non-muddied) supply of the refinisher product.

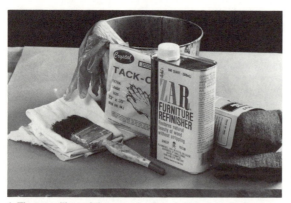

1. First, you'll need these tools, from left to right: lintfree rags, old paintbrush, cheap rubber gloves, tack cloths, clean pail, refinisher, and 3/0 steel wool. Not shown, but smart to have on hand--a plastic dropcloth.

5. Next, author suggests wiping the surfaces off with a clean, lintfree cloth. This is not a step the product makers say is necessary but our expert finds it ensures a clean surface.

6. The procedure often raises the grain (called whiskers by some) if so, use a fine sandpaper (150) to carefully sand the surfaces smooth to the touch. Use light pressure.

7. Dust off all residue using a foxtail or other soft, clean bristle brush. Remove dust from bench surface too.

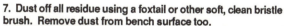

8. For final preparation step, carefully wipe surfaces with a tack cloth. Refold pad as you work.

9. Use your preferred finish to complete the do-over. Here, we simply brushed-on Antique Oil, waited 10 minutes then buffed with a clean, lintfree rag.

After. With dirt-encrusted finish removed the wood's beauty shines through. Test sample shown here took 15 minutes to rejuvenate completely. Conclusion: Refinisher gives excellent results when used for the right chores.

Often, a considerable amount of old finish can be removed while it is dry. Here, poorly adhered lacquer is easily scraped off using a stiff-bladed putty knife. Notice the rounded corners on the knife; this tool was filed at these points to prevent any chance of digging into wood.

Next, Wash the Piece

In most--but not necessarily all--cases it is wisest to follow the solvent bath with a water one. But, be advised that water should be judiciously applied when working with old furniture. For example, too much water on a lacquered or shellacked piece will cause the finish to turn milky white. If you bring on a great deal of discoloration through careless application of water, you may find it necessary to strip the entire finish--when it could have been avoided. Varnish, as mentioned earlier, resists water damage.

A danger that you should be equally aware of is that excessive water on a piece of old furniture can cause structural problems. If water penetrates the glue joints the piece will be wobbly at best, and fall apart at worst. You should know, too, that water on certain raw woods will cause ugly discoloration. If left on oak, for example, water will soon turn the wood a ghastly, mottled black.

If you decide that a mild washing solution is desirable, mix Ivory soap with lukewarm water. Apply this solution to the surface using a cloth, then rinse off the mixture using a cloth and clear lukewarm water. Carefully

Commercial paint remover is applied generously to the surface to be stripped. It is important that you read and follow the manufacturer's instructions for the remover that you bought.

inspect the rinsed piece to make certain that no moisture is left at or in the joints or the glue may become softened.

It is very important that you allow ample drying time between the washing and application of new finish. Though surface water will dry very rapidly, especially if you are working outdoors on a windy day, keep in mind that there is water in those crevices and joints. These areas--as well as raw wood (if any such spots exist on your piece) take much longer to dry completely. Most professionals allow three drying days before proceeding with the next steps.

EVALUATING THE PIECE

Once the piece is thoroughly cleaned it will look dull because you've removed the wax. But it is now that you can carefully and intelligently inspect the furniture so that you can decide just how you will proceed. If the appearance pleases you, that is, there are no excessively worn or stained spots, you can restore the shine by applying a new coat of wax (See Chapter 5). At this time, besides deciding just how you will proceed, you should make a careful examination to determine what, if any, repairs are needed--major or cosmetic.

Now you must decide the best course: 1) leave the piece as is and rewax , 2) work around the existing finish--the usual course with valuable antiques where you do not want to destroy the original, or 3) strip the piece and do a complete refinishing job.

REMOVING THE OLD FINISH--STRIPPING

As mentioned earlier in this book there are basically three methods for removing an old finish--sanding, burning with a torch and commercial remover. Since the first two methods require an inordinate amount of time and effort, we'll stick with the easier--but equally effective--removers. Without a doubt, the commercial removers are the do-it-yourselfer's best bet. Be advised that a quality remover, when used correctly, will let you do the job a great deal faster and with far less frustration.

When working with a paint remover, follow the safety rules outlined here as well as those spelled out by manufacturers on their labels.

- **DO** wear a long-sleeved shirt.

- **DO** wear safety goggles.

- **DO** work in a well-ventilated place.

- **DO** wear rubber gloves.

- **DO** discard dirty rags, newspapers and other contaminated materials in a covered metal container.

- **DON'T** work near an open flame.

- **DON'T** work near spark-producing equipment.

Before you begin the stripping operation, always take the time to remove carefully any hardware or nonfixed

WORKING WITH PAINT STRIPPER

The coated surface is kept wet with remover until the old finish has softened. When removing several layers of stubborn paint, cover the remover with a layer of aluminum foil or plastic to inhibit evaporation and permit remover to penetrate deeper.

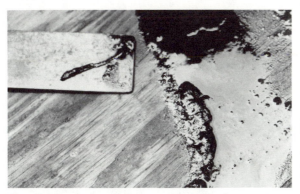

When finish softens and blisters, scrape it off using a putty knife. To minimize chance of damage to the wood, scrape with the grain only, if possible. Keep a pile of old newspapers handy for wiping off the knife after each scraping pass.

Open pores in hardwoods must be cleaned of old finish too. To do it, use 2/0 steel wool saturated with remover; rub hard in direction of grain.

A good professional stunt for getting the finish off a turned leg bottom is to simply stand it in a coffee can half-filled with remover. A wire brush speeds up finish removal on a turning but do take care to avoid damage to the wood. In narrow crevices (V-grooves, etc.) a toothbrush or coarse string is best.

ornamentation. These items are cleaned separately and reinstalled later. It also makes sense to plug screwholes and the like with paper or cloth to save having to hunt for them later (because they're filled with gunk).

Basically, the finish removal operation consists of these steps:

1. Brush on a generous coat of remover with an old paintbrush. Do not brush out the remover too thin or you will lessen its paint-softening ability. If at all possible try to work with a horizontal surface so that the remover can sit and soak rather than run off. If the piece is small enough to handle, you can ensure this by simply rotating it to work one side at a time.

If the latter is impossible and you must work on a vertical plane, use a paste remover which will not run off as fast. Keep in mind that if the remover is not applied thickly and allowed to soak into the finish, you will have to repeat the stripping step. It is very important that you work in a well-ventilated room--even when using a water wash remover. Outdoors is the perfect workshop for stripping but, do not work in direct sunlight or the remover will evaporate too rapidly to soften the finish. At any rate, the remover should never be allowed to dry completely on the surface.

2. 10 minutes or so after application of stripper, the finish will start to blister. Make a test pass with a putty knife to find out whether or not the surface has softened sufficiently. If it has, use a stiff-bladed scraper or putty knife to remove it. Have a generous supply of old newspapers handy for wiping off the knife at frequent intervals or you will be transporting the gook back to the workpiece. As the top sheet of newspaper becomes loaded with softened finish, roll it up and deposit it in a nearby metal trash can. If you are stripping an open-grained hardwood, a little more elbow grease is required. It is a *must* that you get all the finish out of those open pores, discussed earlier; the best way to do this is with 2/0 steel wool saturated with

PRO TRICKS TO SPEED UP STRIPPING

A round file, often called a rattail, works fine for the initial cleaning out of cove portion on this turned leg.

Quick way to clean a tight crevice; fold 100-grit sandpaper as shown here.

For slightly wider crevices try using a narraow strip of burlap (or emery cloth).

Use a 1"-wide strip of emery cloth—shoeshine fashion—on smooth sections of spindle. Take care to avoid making any deep surface scratches by excessive cross-grain sanding.

A great tool for getting softened old finish out of a carving or other ornamentation—an old toothbrush. Sandpaper won't do the job here. (Photograph courtesy Benjamin Moore Co.)

Final cleanup on a leg is easily accomplished with steel wool. The next day, when the piece is completely dry, check for and remove any steel wool particles that remain on the surface.

A hand scraper is a good tool for use on end grain where stain penetration is deep thus hard to get out.

remover. Don't tackle this particular task with a halfhearted effort or the finished product will reflect it. In fact, this rubbing has to be done with considerable pressure. For this reason, whenever possible, do the rubbing with the grain and not across it.

During the scraping-off-the-old- finish stage, all is fair when it comes to picking which tool to use. Items that are normally unrelated to workshop activity can often serve admirably here. Some favored ones include strips of burlap and coarse twine for taking finish off various shapes in turnings; orange sticks, Q-tips and toothbrushes for getting into crevices, ornamental carvings, etc. Use your imagination here; utilize any tool that will make the job easier. The important point here is that you don't want to create any new dents, nicks or scratches in the surface, because they will show through on the new finish.

For this reason, metal objects should be used with care; even steel wool, which can be a great help when cleaning rounded surfaces on legs, can do considerable damage if it is too coarse, or rubbed too vigorously across the grain. When it comes to choosing a steel wool for the strippping operation, stick with either 1/0 or 2/0. The finer grades will require an excessive amount of rubbing while the coarser ones will probably scratch the wood below.

Sandpaper can and should be used to help remove a stubborn finish. It is particularly helpful for large flat areas, and for getting into corners. To prevent rounding over edges or dishing in flat areas, work with the sandpaper wrapped around a backup block.

3. When the finish has been removed to your satisfaction, you must neutralize the piece to halt the chemical action. To do it, you will need either lacquer thinner, or turpentine, so check the label when you buy the remover. (If using a water wash remover read the following section.)

No matter the solvent used, rub it onto the surface using 2/0 steel wool, working with the grain whenever possible. After neutralizing, let the piece dry at least 24 hours before proceeding with sanding.

Water-wash removers

These are applied in the same fashion as removers which must be neutralized with solvent. The big difference is that scraping can sometimes be eliminated. If you are working outdoors, once the surface is softened employ a strong jet of water from the garden hose to wash off the piece. If you are working in an unfinished basement, it is a must that there be a floor drain for water and waste to wash into; the scum can be cleaned out later. If you are working inside without a floor drain, water-wash remover can be removed by using a large sponge and pail of clean water. Frequently dip the sponge into the water to clean it; when the water becomes too muddied to clear the sponge when it's dipped, change it.

Water-wash removers offer the obvious advantage of saving time and some arm power. But, in my opinion, the disadvantages are twofold: 1) they do not remove old finishes as thoroughly as the solvent type and 2) the risk of damage from too much water is considerable. You should know that excessive water

on an old piece can and often does cause damage. For example, genuinely antique pieces are *not* joined with waterproof glue. Thus, there is strong chance that a shower from the hose will weaken joints by softening glue. An even worse result can be the delamination of veneers and inlays, quite possibly to the degree that they are beyond repair.

Advice: Only use a water-wash remover when you are absolutely certain that the piece cannot be damaged by water; don't let the fact that it is a simpler method be your only guide when choosing your remover. Also, when using a water wash remover, make it your habit to work quickly. Immediately after hosing off a piece, wipe it with paper towels or clean absorbent rags. *DO NOT* put the piece in the sun to dry.

ABOUT STRIPPING

Since evaporation works against the stripper, many experienced refinishers slow it down by covering the coated surface with aluminum foil or sheet plastic immediately after application. This technique is especially helpful when removing two or more layers of finish because it lets the remover eat deeper.

For several reasons, after stripping you are well-advised to sand the entire piece with a medium-fine sandpaper. The most important reason for this is to ensure that the following stain will be absorbed evenly by the wood. Equally important is the knowledge that heavy rubbing with steel wool--which often takes place during stripping--can, in effect, polish the wood. Where wood has been polished by steel wool it will take stain differently than the unpolished areas will. You should know that light rubbing with steel wool *does not* cause polishing--only heavy rubbing does. To learn the look, rub scrap raw walnut with steel wool, in two different spots, using heavy and light strokes.

Once all of the finish has been removed and the piece has been neutralized, set it aside for at least one day so that it can dry completely. If a water-wash stripper was used, allow two-days.

ABOUT STUBBORN PAINTS

Called refractory paint (but more commonly known as milk paint), these stubborn finishes, which are found on many older pieces, often resist even today's commercial paint removers. They consist of a penetrating red paint made by mixing together red pigment (iron oxide) with skim milk or buttermilk.

A hundred or so years ago, this paint was considered desirable; it covered knots and other imperfections and gave a visual effect not unlike cherry or mahogany. Other colors were made by varying the pigments; e.g., using lamp black, sienna, or green instead of iron oxide.

A refractory paint is particularly difficult to remove from wood because it penetrates deep into the wood pores. Further, it leaves a stain that is even more difficult to remove.

Removing a Refractory Paint and Its Stain

The general procedure followed by most professionals is:

- Remove the refractory paint using one of the methods discussed earlier.

- Keep surface completely wet with remover as you are stripping it off.

- Treat the stain with denatured alcohol; make certain the surface is kept wet with alcohol as you rub with 2/0 steel wool.

If stain persists: Working outdoors, on concrete for water runoff, apply a sal soda (washing) solution. To make the sal soda solution, mix 1 lb. sal soda in 5 qts. hot water. Do not inhale the fumes as you mix the solution. Apply the solution with a mop and allow it to stand for 15 minutes. Scrub with a brush then rinse well with clear water; wipe off, and allow the piece to dry (out of the sun).

Caution: Do not use sal soda on mahogany, cherry, rosewood or veneers (water softens the glue in veneered pieces).

STRIPPING BY A PROFESSIONAL

Because stripping an old piece of furniture is the least happy part of refinishing, many prefer to take their old furniture to a professional stripping shop for this step. Professional stripping shops are opening up in increasing numbers around the country. Many of them are franchised, which means that the operator is a licensed dealer using a stripping method developed by a large company. Smaller local operations are usually by an individual who does the work using a personally preferred method.

Most professional strippers use either one of two methods to do the job:

- *Cold tank stripping* Generally more expensive than the hot-tank process, but it is the method to opt for if your piece has inlays and veneers. In cold-tank stripping the furniture is dipped into a tankful of chemical solvent that consists, basically, of methylene chloride.

- *Hot-tank stripping* In this process, glue can be-- and often is--attacked. And although damage to glue joints in solid-wood furniture is generally minimal, it can be severe with more delicate pieces. Veneers have been damaged beyond repair and inlays have been known to literally fall apart.

In hot-tank dipping, caustic soda mixed with water in a large tank is heated to a temperature between 140° and 170°F. The furniture is immersed in this solution until the finish is softened. When it is removed from the tank it is rinsed with a high-pressure hose. Next, it is dunked into a muriatic acid bath and, finally, it is given a second rinsing.

Since caustic soda is capable of dissolving any organic matter left immersed too long, it is important that you pick a stripper who keeps his mind on the task at hand. Careless stripping can usually be seen in places where the softer pulp areas have been eaten out while the harder areas (annual rings) remain intact as ridges. There are plenty of first-rate strippers, make sure you pick one.

STRIPPING PENETRATING RESINS

These extra-tough finishes impregnate the wood and give it a hard plastic surface. Because penetration is so deep into the wood, the finish is a particularly durable one and extremely difficult, if not impossible, to remove completely. You can try removal by sanding but it will require sanding off an excessive amount of wood--because of that deep penetration. Chemical remover alone will not remove these finishes. Your best bet with a penetrating-resin finish is to go over it with another coat of the same material. Before you do, however, give the surface a light sanding with fine sandpaper, dust it off and wipe with a tack rag.

BLEACHING

Bleaching is necessary only when you must lighten the color of the wood or remove a stain. Until recently, oxalic-acid was a popular wood bleaching chemical but the Environmental Protection Agency changed that by banning the further sale of the chemical. Though you can work with a household bleach, it is generally best to use a commercially prepared bleach (available at paint stores). Most of these are two-part solutions which are either intermixed or applied in steps.

Here are two bleaching methods to try:

- *Household bleach* (such as Purex or Clorox) These will remove some chemicals, dyes and ink but not all of the spots you are likely to encounter. You can try bleaching first with one of these and, if the stain is stubborn, switch to one of the commercial two-parters.

To use household bleach, apply it full strength (unless a weaker, water-thinned solution is desirable) using a brush or cloth. Watch for results, which should begin almost immediately. Within five minutes you should be able to see what will be the final results. To slow down the bleaching action, wash the surface with clear water. For greater lightening, apply more bleach. When satisfied, halt the bleaching action by neutralizing with a solution of equal parts vinegar and water. Make certain the piece is completely dry before proceeding with finishing.

- *Commercial two-part bleaches* The instructions for using one of these is always spelled out on the label; make certain you read and understand them before proceeding. In general, solution number one is applied with either clean cloth or sponge and allowed to set for a specified time--often five minutes for softwoods, a little longer for hardwoods. Solution number two is then applied while solution number one is still wet. (With some brands, the mixing is done before applying the bleach to the wood.) The piece is then set aside and allowed to dry for at least 12 hours. When the bleached surface is completely dry it is sanded lightly to remove chemical salt residue from it. If a still-lighter shade of wood is desired, the two-step bleaching process must be repeated. And, usually with commercial bleaches when two or more bleach applications are required, the bleach must be neutralized. Often this is done with a solution of one part vinegar to two parts water--but check the label.

PREPARING A MILD HOMEMADE BLEACH

You can mix a bleach of your own using oxalic acid crystals or powder (available at paint and hardware stores) and tartaric acid powder (from a drugstore). If you decide to make your own bleach, mix the solution in a glass jar or enamel container. If it is to be stored, affix a **POISON** label.

Making the bleach

1. Put 2 rounded tbsp. each of oxalic acid crystals and tartaric acid powder in a glass jar. (2 tbsp. equal approx. 2 ozs.)
2. Pour 1 qt. hot water over crystals to dissolve them.
3. Use the solution hot; if it has been stored, reheat it.

Using the bleach

1. Apply the hot solution to the entire surface using a small cloth. Concentrate on the stained area, but keep the entire surface wet.
2. As you apply the solution, rearrange the cloth frequently to assure application with a clean section of the wet cloth.
3. Allow the bleach to work on a section for 20 minutes.
4. To stop the bleaching action, wash off the bleach with a neutralizing solution of 1 tbsp. of clear ammonia mixed in 1 qt. water.
5. Wipe off the neutralizer with clean cloth repeatedly dunked into clean water and wrung out. Finish wiping with clean, dry cloths.
6. Let the piece dry for 24 hrs. and then reinspect the piece. If dark spots persist, repeat the bleach steps and neutralize a second time.

Some Words of Caution

Since various bleaches can cause damage to skin and eyes, do wear rubber gloves and goggles when working with them. Added precaution: Read the label safety instructions. If you should get any of the chemicals on your skin or in your eyes, immediately give the affected area a thorough rinsing with clear, cold water for 15 minutes. If any chemical gets into your eyes call your doctor.

Keep in mind that the raised grain that you will be sanding next has in it a certain amount of dried chemicals from all those steps you've just gone through. Thus, the dust created by sanding may be irritating to your skin, lungs, and eyes. For your protection and comfort, wear a breathing mask (respirator), goggles, and a long-sleeved shirt when sanding a recently-stripped project.

Now you are at square one if you are rejuvenating an old piece. That is, you are at the same stage you would be at if you had bought a piece of unfinished furniture. In the following chapter we will start looking at making

minor repairs. But first, some important information about that 20th century wood product--plywood.

PLYWOOD
Plywood grades

All plywood is graded at the mill. The grades help you choose the right plywood for the job at hand whether it is building a new project or repairing an old piece of furniture. Basically, there are four plywood grades you should, know about:

• **A** is basically a flawless surface.

• **B** is almost flawless, but usually has some patches.

• **C** has patches and some knots.

• **D** usually has a considerable number of both patches and knots.

Plywood sheets are designated as A-C, A-B, and so forth. This tells you the grade on both sides. Thus, if both sides of a sheet will be visible in the finished project, it is advisable to buy A-A plywood. On the other hand, if one side will not show at all, as with a countertop, you can save a considerable amount of money because you will be able to use the A-D sheet and hide the D side.

Plywood Surface Preparation

For most applications, the sanding that the plywood gets at the mill makes the material smooth enough for project use. Generally, it is drum-sanded to about the equivalent of 3/0 abrasive. You can, of course, sand it still smoother but make certain you use a sanding backup block or a pad sander. Keep in mind that those soft, light-colored areas can be dished out if they are sanded excessively and carelessly. Plywood, if desired, can be given a coat of sanding sealer prior to sanding, to help tame wild grain by ensuring a more even distribution of stain. You can make your own sealer coat using 3-lb. cut waterwhite shellac thinned 1 part shellac to 8 parts denatured alcohol. A sanding sealer helps minimize the possibility of dishing out the softwood areas, too.

Patching Plywood

Often, the easiest way to repair a damaged section of plywood is by removing and replacing the damaged portion of the top ply, or veneer. To do it, use a sharp utility knife or razor blade, and steel straightedge to make a neat cutout. Cut away only as much surface veneer as is necessary to correct the fault. When all four sides have been sliced--through the top ply--use a sharp chisel to carefully remove the rectangular blemished area. Cut a new piece of matching veneer (plywood) taking care to match the grain as closely as possible with the original piece, and glue it in using carpenter's glue. Clamp until dry. To prevent any chance of the patch-piece sticking to the clamp pad cover the patch with wax paper before clamping.

4

MINOR REPAIRS, STAINING, AND FILLING

A very important part of any refinishing project is the treatment and repair of nicks, dents, scratches, parts looseness and the like. The same thing holds true for finishing a brand new piece of unfinished furniture, particularly if you treated yourself to one of the many fine kits now on the market. Kit work, of course, is not repair work but, assembling a kit correctly and preparing it for finishing falls into the same category of workshop task. Many repair chores on older furniture are often, simply, cosmetic repairs: Frequently, after a thorough cleaning, a piece can be almost immediately returned to use after correcting minor flaws or problems. Hiding scratches, removing blemishes, etc. are typical cosmetic repairs. Sometimes, even regluing a wobbly leg takes no more effort than a cosmetic repair does.

At any rate, the answers to most of the repair problems you are likely to encounter will be found in these pages. If you come across more serious problems that you don't feel comfortable handling, chances are the piece of furniture should be brought to a professional repair shop for treatment.

Though you should have some knowledge of the woods and materials used in most furniture, there really is no need to memorize such information in order to do a credible repair, refinishing or finishing job. Instead, you need on hand a good reference source for quick perusal and reference--each time you are faced with a challenge. This book gives you that tool.

GLUING

The majority of repair jobs are gluing jobs. Thus, it is safe to assume that glue properly applied and left to dry under the right conditions (i.e., under pressure) is the best way to ensure a lasting repair. Typical repairs that are made with glue include replacing spindles, closing a gap or joint in a wide surface such as seat or top, strengthening loose corners and so on.

Rules for gluing: Before starting any glue repair job,

learn the general rules for gluing. By following the accepted guidelines, your repairs are sure to last;

• It is imperative that all surfaces to be joined be clean and dry. If necessary, use a dull knife or stiff-bladed putty knife to scrape away all traces of the old dried glue, finish and dirt. Since many furniture glues can be softened by exposure to moisture, heat some vinegar and, with a stiff brush, vigorously scrub this on any glue-encrusted surface you plan to reglue.

• Do all your gluing in a dry, warm room (about 70°-75° F).

• Surfaces to be glued one to the other must be properly fitted. Use a plane, file and sandpaper to smooth any uneven surfaces. Bear in mind that smooth surfaces hold best. Think of the times two pieces of glass were stacked, and you could not separate them easily. The smoothness of the surfaces themselves provide some degree of holding power. When mating surfaces are ready to be joined, give both a final light, sanding with a 100-grit or finer abrasive. This will increase the glue's holding power.

Applying glue: Depending upon the glue you prefer to work with, application may vary slightly. So, when using a glue for the first time, do read the instruction label to make sure you apply it correctly. In general, however, here is the gluing procedure you will follow most often:

• Apply a thin layer of glue to both surfaces to be joined. <u>Important</u>: Less is more, do not overdo it when applying glue.

• Immediately spread the glue evenly. Use a small stick, spatula or brush. In this step, it is common to remove all excess thus, minimize glue squeezeout.

• Allow the glue to be exposed to the air for several minutes so it has a chance to become tacky.

• Next, press the pieces together and, using a water-dampened cloth, immediately wipe off all glue squeezeout.

PRO TIP ---a word about squeezeout. *Any glue that squeezes onto the wood surface will seal the wood below it from accepting stain. The result, a white spot in your stained piece.* **Do Not** *wipe glue squeezeout with a wet cloth unless you plan to paint the piece. Most professionals minimize squeezeout by using a scant amount of glue. Then, should a glue line appear as clamp pressure is applied, it is left alone---not wiped off. Instead, this glue is permitted to set to a semi-dry, half-hardened state. It is then carefully scraped off with a sharp chisel or razor blade. Your best bet? Do some tests on scrap wood.*

• Apply pressure, using either clamps or rope. When such pressure is applied, there will be additional glue squeezeout; per the previous paragraph, make your choice as to course of action for squeezeout.

• Before you set the piece aside to dry, check to make certain that all parts are aligned perfectly and fit together as they should. Remember, once that glue dries the shape will be permanent and parts adjustment will be impossible.

• Set the piece aside for 24 hrs. to dry.

Clamping action

There's no doubt that putting pressure on a glued joint is the surest way to success. But the pressure must be applied while the glue is drying--or the bond won't last. There are a wide variety of clamps available for use on furniture (see chapter one); your local hardware dealer should be able to help you pick the right one for the job at hand. Regardless of type of clamp used, make certain you protect the workpiece

To repair a split in this softwood (pine) tabletop, the crack is first spread with carpenter's glue. Then, pressure to close the joint is applied using a pair of bar clamps. Small finishing nails are then driven at an angle, through predrilled holes, from opposite sides of the crack. Finally, glue squeeze-out will be removed with a damp cloth and the set nails will be concealed with a putty stick.

from clamp marks use pads of folded newspapers or wood blocks between clamp jaws and workpiece.

You can improvise a clamp by creating a tourniquet of cloth or rope. Applied properly, a tourniquet gives

even pressure and is especially helpful when regluing chairs or table legs. The way to do it is to wind the rope twice around the glued section as close as possible to the repair. Then a stick is inserted between the two ropes and turned until all slack is taken up and the parts are securely held. One end of the stick is then slipped under the seat or tabletop to keep it from springing loose and causing unwinding.

Pressure can be applied to flat surfaces by placing on a considerable amount of weight. A stack of books on a repaired section of veneer, will often produce adequate results.

HARDWARE FOR REPAIRS

Often, it is wise to give glue an assist by using some hardware when repairing a wide crack, weak corner, or the like. Of several types available, those commonly used in furniture repairs are called mending plates and

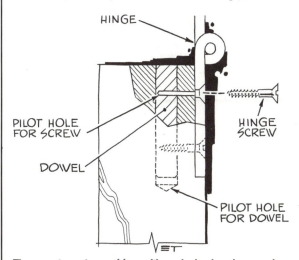

The surest way to provide positive gripping by a loosened screw, or screw that must be turned into end-grain, is to install a dowel in a hole bored across the original screwhole. The dowel is installed permanently using glue and allowed to dry completely before reboring the screw pilot hole. Now, the screw will be firmly anchored in the hardwood dowel.

Cabinet scraper lets you get a smooth finish fast. They're available at most hardware stores and craftsman supply houses. See appendix.

corner braces. The first type is a piece of flat metal with configurations such as T,L and I. Countersunk holes are bored through for using screws to hold the hardware. A corner brace is, basically, a mending plate that's been bent at a 90° angle so that it can be used on an inside corner. A corner brace is also predrilled to accept screws.

A metal brace should be installed after the defect has been cleaned out, spread with glue and clamped. While the work is clamped, the iron is positioned to straddle the defect then, permanently installed using appropriate-size screws. It is a must, of course, to bore pilot holes in the wood to receive the plate-holding screws. Even when you install a brace or iron, leave the clamps in place for 24 hrs.

LARGE HOLES

Large surface holes and cracks can be patched using one of the many wood doughs, putties, or plastic-type wood fillers available these days. Since you are likely to be faced with a mountain of wood fillers in paint or hardware store, do take the time to read labels, to make certain you get the one that will do your job. Some fillers come premixed, ready to use; others are in powder form which must be mixed with water to a workable consistency. Although manufacturers are inclined to make claims to the contrary, these generally do not take stains the same way as the surrounding wood. In my experience, I have yet to come across a wood filler that truly accepts stain and makes a spot invisible. Happily, there are tricks for making your patch job a pretty respectable one.

Wood dough is a fine filler for use on a surface to be painted. To use it, first clean out the hole thoroughly, then with a putty knife or spatula work the dough into the hole. Make certain it is packed tightly. Work quickly and without interruption since the material usually becomes tougher to handle the longer it is exposed to the air. After filling the hole, immediately wipe off any excess dough. Since most patch fillers shrink somewhat as they dry, you can use either of two methods to compensate for this characteristic: leave the dough-filled hole a bit higher than the surrounding wood surface and sand it flush when dry or, leave the application flush and when it dries, fill the resulting depression with more wood dough. Using the latter method usually requires three or four applications before the repaired area no longer shrinks below the surrounding area. If you opt for the first method, however, make certain you exercise care when sanding the convex surface so you do not damage the surrounding wood.

In general, it is better to mix stain with wood doughs and patch fillers before using either. Done this way you can test the color on scrap or in an inconspicuous spot to see just how close you have come to matching the piece being repaired.

FINAL REMINDER: A wood-patch filler is *not* a paste wood filler. I have no intention of "beating a dead horse" by stating this again but, I have on so many occasions seen a paint store clerk mislead a customer

on these products that I want to make certain that those who bought this book know the distinction. If you're still confused about the two materials, please refer to the Paste Wood Filler information in Chapter 2.

WARPS

A warp in a board can occasionally be removed, or at the least minimized, by thoroughly soaking the board, although this is not always successful. If possible, remove the culprit from the furniture piece and work on it separately. The usual procedure is to wet the board completely with water then place it convex side down on wet canvas. Next, the board is weighted with heavy objects. Keep the board wet until maximum straightening has been achieved. Replace the board on the piece while still damp; use screws to hold it there. As it dries, the abutting pieces, to which it has been fastened, should help deter it from going back to a warped condition.

But, make no mistake about it, straightening a warped or cupped board is no simple task. If the quick method discussed above does not work--and the piece is a valuable one--you might be better off consulting with a local professional woodworker. There are some other stunts that can be performed but they do require special skills and knowledge.

DENTS

Often, a small dent can be removed by using a steam iron. Such dents usually occur when a piece of furniture is struck by a rigid item (e.g.; something dropped onto a surface). As a result, the wood fibers in the banged area are bent out of shape. Sometimes, treatment with a steam iron returns those fibers to normal, or near-normal, position.
Here's how to iron out a dent:

• Thoroughly dampen a clean cloth and position it over the dented area.

• With the iron set on *synthetics*, place it on the cloth until the latter begins to dry. Check periodically to make certain that you are not damaging the surrounding surface.

• When the cloth becomes dry, check the dent with both fingertips and eye to see if the fibers have returned to normal position. If not repeat procedure.
Note: When steaming hardwood, make several pinholes, 1/4" deep, in the dented area. These will permit more steam to enter into the denser woods.
Caution: You can cause damage by excessive steaming, i.e.; steam will attack both water-soluble glues and veneers. Do not use this technique when either is present.

OTHER MINOR REPAIRS

Sticking and ill-fitting drawers are common maladies old funiture. Oftentimes, it seems to take a near-genius mentality to remove a stubborn, sticking drawer from its berth but, what is really needed is a great deal of patience. Sometimes you can reach in your arm and aim a squirt or two of silicone spray on the drawer slides and runners. But it is not uncommon for a careful inspection to reveal that a nail or screw is holding the drawer fast. For this reason, brute strength alone in backing out a stuck drawer is ill-advised.

Once you get the drawer out--this may require carefully removing the carcase back--make a careful inspection to determine why it sticks. The first, and obvious, is to look in the carcase to see if a loose item has fallen from this drawer or a drawer above to cause the jamming. If all is clear, are the drawer runners intact and smooth? Or, are they missing or swollen? Or, is the sticking caused by the furniture itself? Is the carcase out-of-square? If so, it is probably pinching and holding fast the drawer as it is inserted.

Replace the drawer runners if they are worn excessively (use hardwood). Apply either a liberal dose of paste wax or silicone spray to runners. If the chest is seriously out-of-square, you have a major project ahead of you. The piece will have to be taken apart and reassembled perfectly square. The same holds true for a drawer, if it is out of whack. Whether you must take apart the drawer or carcase, do so carefully. Clean all old glue from joints and reassemble the piece using glue and screws, through predilled (pilot) holes. Always use clamps to hold the parts tightly until the glue dries. Clean all dirt buildup off the drawer and spray the slides and bottom with silicone spray before reinstalling the drawer in the cabinet.

LOOSE SCREWS

More often then not, these are usually the culprits when you have a hinge problem. It is also common in plate-holding hardware (i.e., pulls) and failure is generally due to abuse, misuse and rough treatment over the years. In many cases with a loose screw in furniture you will not be able to solve the problem by simply replacing the screw with a longer one--because the screw is generally into just 3/4" thick wood. Several tricks for tightening up loose screws include:

• Fill the hole with glue and toothpicks, wood splinters, etc. When dry, reinsert the screw.

• Fill the hole with either a plastic wood patch, wood dough or epoxy putty. When dry, bore an undersize pilot hole, then reinstall the screw.

• If the surrounding wood is in bad shape--and won't provide adequate hold for screw threads--your best bet may be to bore a hole at a right angle to the screw axis and glue-in a dowel, as shown in the picture on the facing page. Rebore the screw's pilot hole--which will now pass through the dowel--and run in the screw. The screw will now be anchored in the dowel.

WHITE SPOTS AND RINGS

More often than not, these are found on a piece with a shellac finish. Since most liquids will cause damage to shellac, it makes sense to keep such pieces well-waxed. If the white ring--the type caused by a wet cup or glass--is hazy and not clearly defined, you may be able to remove it by scrubbing with an abrasive mixture of cigarette ash mixed with fresh lemon juice.

If this is unsuccessful, try rubbing very lightly with 3/0 steel wool and oil (either lemon or boiled linseed). This will take off most white spots; the more stubborn ones can be coaxed a little more by adding a little table salt.

For a super-stubborn white spot, you will probably have to resort to a pumice mixture. Mix the pumice (available at paint stores) with a litttle water and apply it to the spot along with a little oil, as before. Use a padded block behind the steel wool to prevent any chance of digging-in with fingers. Rub with care so as to avoid any damage to surrounding surfaces.

There are some commercial products made for this purpose; you may want to consult with your paint store dealer. If the piece is valuable and you feel your skills are limited, it might be best to call in a professional furniture finisher.

SCRATCHES

If the piece has been waxed regularly, chances are any scratches will be merely surface scratches. These are fairly easy to remove using one of the commercially available furniture cleaner-conditioners. Minor scratches can be concealed using such household items as coffee, tea, shoe polish--even a stain that is made with tobacco. Here you can turn your imagination loose to pick whatever will let you come the closest to matching the piece's color.

To repair a deep scratch use one the of the wax crayonlike sticks that are sold for use on prefinished paneling. Happily, several different sticks can be mixed and blended to match just about any color on any piece of furniture.

SANDING AND ABRASIVES

Though every phase in refinishing or finishing is important, you can be sure that none is more important than the sanding that you will give the bare wood. This step, to a great degree, will determine just how professional-looking your effort will turn out. And, bare wood will always need sanding: whether you just stripped the finish from an old piece, or bought a brand new piece of unfinished furniture, you can expect to have do some smoothing.

Thus, regardless of what type project yours is, it is in your best interests to take the time to learn the basics of what a good sanding job is all about. The following will provide all you need to know, and you do not even have to bother yourself with memorizing the lesser details. You can always quickly find the information, before shopping for supplies, by checking the index. Or, if it will help you, take the book with you when you go to do your buying. At any rate, here's a rundown on those coated abrasives you should be familiar with:

• The *flint* abrasive papers--commonly called sandpaper--are inexpensive and generally of poor quality when compared with the other types. They wear out quickly and the backing fails rapidly when they're used on pad sanders. Both *aluminum oxide* and *garnet* papers cost a bit more, but their longer use-spans make the extra pennies a smart investment. Though primarily intended for use on metal, flexible emery cloth is a desirable abrasive for a woodworker to keep on hand for use on turnings, especially.

About Paper Backings

The backings on which the abrasives are affixed are rated according to flexibility: "A" is a flexible finishing paper, "C" and "D" are for cabinet work, and "E" is for machine sanding, where heat generated by the speed at which the paper travels calls for extra toughness. There is also a cloth backing rated "J" for hand work and "X" for power sanding.

Open and Closed Coats

This refers to the amount of grits covering the backing paper. Most of the papers you will be concerned with are produced in two coats:

• *Open coat* paper has abrasive grains covering from 50 to 70 percent of the backing. The greater spaces between the grains is intended to help prevent clogging, especially when the abrasive is used on painted surfaces or softwoods.

• *Closed coat* paper means that the grits cover the entire backing paper. This type is intended for those surfaces that will not clog papers quickly--i.e., hardwoods and certain metals and plastics. Closed coat papers cut at a greater speed than open coat, but they also clog (fill) a lot quicker thus, become useless.

Using Coated Abrasives

Stated extra-simply--you start with a coarse abrasive and you finish with a fine one, generally using a number of grades in between the two extremes. This does not mean that you should automatically run out and buy the coarsest abrasive you can lay your hands on. On furniture projects you should start with a coarse grade, such as 1/2, that will let you level the surface without scratching it. Remember that if you sand scratches into the wood it is you who will have to remove them. The accepted practice is to smooth the wood further by switching to a medium grade paper (1/0 to 3/0), then finish with a fine-grade paper (6/0 to 8/0).

Sanding can be done by hand or with power but, the latter saves a great deal of time and effort. And, to avoid any chance of damaging a surface with a power sander, a first-time user should practice with both pad or belt sander before touching the power tool to the actual project. Read the toolmaker's instructions for use and safety rules. Finally, both sanders are fairly easy tools to master; it just takes some plain, old-fashioned common sense.

Good sanding practices

Here are some tips for making your sanding time happier--and more successful:

• Always sand wood with the grain--not across it--if

Abrasives Comparisons Chart			
GRIT	O-SYMBOL	DESCRIPTION	USES
400 360	10/0 none	Extra fine	Used for rubbing varnish and lacquer top coats to obtain a rubbed look.
280 240 220	8/0 7/0 6/0	Very fine	Finish-sand undercoat and top coat. Final sanding on raw hardwoods.
180 150	00000 0000	Fine	Final sanding of raw softwoods.
120 100 80	000 00 0	Medium	Preliminary sanding of bare wood. Also, for first sanding of previous paint.
60 50 40	1/2 1 1-1/2	Coarse	Initial rough sanding and for paint and finish removing.

This chart gives a comparison of the various abrasive coatings. There are coarser grades made, but these are generally not used in furniture making or finishing.

possible. In those instances when cross-grain sanding is unavoidable, do it with fine paper and light pressure. Make it a point to stop every so often and to inspect the surface using a bright lamp, to make certain you are not sanding-in scratches.

• When sanding flat surfaces by hand, always use a backup block. That is, wrap the sandpaper around a small block of wood which will prevent you from sanding (rounding) over corners.

• Use straight strokes with even pressure throughout the stroke. On wood, you should never work with a circular or diagonal (to the wood's grain) motion.

• You can lengthen the useful life of a sheet of sandpaper by cleaning it periodically as you work. To do so, tap the sanding block against the floor or workbench so that dust clogging the abrasive will fall away. Some softwoods will clog the paper to such a degree that it may be necessary to clean the abrasive with a stiff brush.

• As you switch from one grade paper to the next finer, clean off all surfaces being worked before starting with the new abrasive grade. Use a vacuum cleaner to remove fine dust to avoid breathing these particles.

• You can make an abrasive more pliable for sanding curved surfaces by first dipping it in turpentine. Do this to make such pesky sanding chores more bearable.

PRO TIP *Many students have asked why a perfectly smooth piece of raw wood will feel "rough" to the touch after the stain is applied. The answer is that the dampness caused by the stain swells the fibers thus, "raises whiskers". Professionals avoid this nuisance at the finishing stage by making their last sanding of the raw wood a wet one. I make a mild soapy solution of warm water and Ivory soap, (the latter serves as a lubricant for the sandpaper) and wipe it on the wood. The water, in effect, imitates the stain. I sand the whiskers off using a fine waterproof paper, either 180 or 220 grit. Now, when the stain is applied, no whiskers will be raised.*

How do I know when to switch from one grade of sandpaper to the next finer one? Good question--and it's the sandpaper question that I have probably been asked by students and magazine readers writing in, more than all other sanding questions combined. The answer is when the paper you are currently using no longer removes stock. Over and above that, after dusting off the particles, run your fingertips over the surface; they'll tell you more about smoothness than your eyes will.

Steel   Wool

To obtain an especially smooth finish, you must finish by rubbing the piece with steel wool. In fact, if you want a high gloss finish, a satin-smooth wood surface is a must. As with coated abrasives, steel wool comes in a variety of grades, from coarse to very fine. In general, grade 1 is usually the coarsest grade ever used on a furniture project. To start, stick with that grade. Continue rubbing, switching to the next finer grade as the job demands.

Steel Wool Grades		
4/0 3/0	Superfine Extra fine	For high final finish.
2/0 0	Fine	General smoothing.
1/0	Medium	Used for finish removal.

These are the steel wool grades used in furniture finishing and refinishing projects. The coarser grades, 2 and 3, are too rough for use on fine furniture woods and should be avoided.

STAINING

The object of stain is to darken wood. Though I have observed that many people seem to be mystified by stains, there is actually no reason to fear using a stain. Actually, you should think of stain as thinned paint--which is exactly what it is.

Basically, a stain is used for one of four reasons:

• To darken a wood in order to place extra emphasis on its grain pattern.

• To try to make one type of wood look like another. For example, birch can often be stained to closely resemble cherry.

• When you control its application, you can create a uniform color on a piece which is made up of several different kinds of wood--like the table on page 19.

• Lastly, to darken or tint repaired and patched areas so that the repair closely matches the original piece.

Types of stains

Because there are a number of types of stains available, I suspect that the variety confuses many. For this reason, I strongly recommend that all do-it-yourselfers pick a favorite type of stain and then stick with it. This reduces the chance of errors creeping into your project.   Also, as you gain familiarity and confidence with your choice, you will increase your mastery of that stain; the net result is that your projects should get better and better looking.

Here the six types of stain you can choose from:

• Penetrating resin

• Water stains

• Pigmented oil (wiping) stains

• NGR stains

• Padding stains

• Varnish and lacquer stains

All of them do what a good stain is supposed to do; the important difference is in how they are worked. Some are easier to use than others and some, in my opinion, should be avoided entirely by amateur finishers. Here's a brief rundown on the six:

• **Penetrating resin** is considered by many to be an easy stain to work with, primarily because it is a finish *system.* You apply the stain, follow with a coat of wax and the job is finished. Since it is a system, and not just a stain, penetrating resin is somewhat like a varnish except that instead of lying on the surface, it sinks deep into the wood pores. Because it is a tough finish it is commonly used on floors.   Penetrating resin is the type finish preferred by many professionals, and probably totally ignored by an equal number. It has its pluses, not the least of which is the toughness which it imparts to the wood to which it is applied. There are many brands available; a few immediately recognizable names are Watco, Clear Rez and Clear Minwax.

Application is fast when you can work with the surface in a horizontal position. Pour a goodly amount of the liquid on the surface and mop it about with rags or large brushes. Some even prefer working this stuff with their hands. The stain is then permitted to soak in for anywhere from 30 to 60 minutes, depending upon how dark you want the piece to look. You then wipe off all excess stain. If you prefer lighter-toned wood, stop here. For a darker finish, apply a second coat within four hours of the first one. The first coat will be pretty much absorbed into the wood by this time. When the second application is completely dry, the piece can be waxed. That's it.

If you decide that this is the type of finish that you want to work with, carefully read the label on the can in the store--*the label must say penetrating resin.*

HOW TO USE A PASTE WOOD FILLER

Paste wood filler comes in a can like this. To use it, see instructions in text and photo captions. *Beware*: Many paint store clerks do not know the difference between paste wood filler and plastic wood patch but you will know, after you've read this book, that there is, indeed, a big difference. To be safe, order by brand. Shown is the brand that author uses—Benwood Paste Wood Filler by Benjamin Moore Paint Company. For use, filler is thinned to the consistency of heavy cream using turpentine.

Let the surface stand undisturbed until the liquid flats out, that is, loses its shine. This usually takes 20-30 minutes.

As described in the text, all open pore wood, such as walnut shown here, requires use of paste wood filler. Here, the neutral filler is being tinted using the same stain that was used on the furniture.

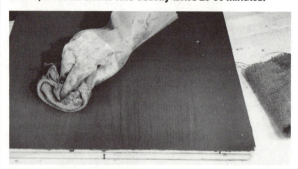

Next, use a coarse rag—burlap is perfect—to remove the filler. First rub across the grain forcing filler into pores; then finish by wiping in grain direction with a clean cloth.

Work only a small area at a time; apply the filler using with-the-grain strokes.

Then rub the brush across the grain to ensure liquid being forced in to the wood's pores.

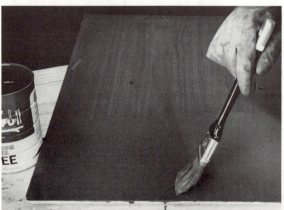

• **Water stains**, in most cases should be avoided by beginning do-it-yourselfers. These come in aniline dye powder form--the stain dyes the wood fibers just as a cloth is dyed. A disadvantage with water stains is that they swell the wood fibers and cause excessive grain raising. Some water stains can be mixed with alcohol to produce a nongrain-raising effect.

Another disadvantage is that the water in the stain can also attack glue in the piece. Thus it should not be used on veneers. The third strike against water stains is that very few retail stores carry them at all. If you must use a water stain, chances are you will have to order it from a craftsman supply house.

• **Pigmented oil (wiping) stains** are the type that I recommend to students in my woodworking class to use. Purists will immediately leap to debate that statement because many of them feel that oil stains hide too much of the grain. Hogwash: The only place I have seen that argument is in a magazine or newspaper article, generally written by a deskbound finisher--that is, a person who rarely, if ever, puts stain on a piece of wood. The professionals I have worked with have shelves filled with oil stains (and so do I).

Handled correctly, an oil stain will bring out grain details as beautifully as any of its counterparts. And because it is far easier to control, you stand a very good chance of doing your best staining with an oil stain. Even if you allow the piece too get too dark it can be lightened with a minimum amount of effort by rubbing with a turpentine-soaked rag, or by sanding when dry.

To use an oil stain, wipe off the smoothed surface with a clean cloth dampened with turpentine. Then wipe the entire surface with a tack rag. You can apply oil stain using either a brush or rag. Allow it to set for about 10 minutes, time depends upon how dark you want the piece. (Note: If you're not sure about this, after five minutes wipe off the stain. If it's too light, another coat can be applied to darken.) At any rate, after about 10 minutes, start wiping off all excess, non-absorbed stain, with clean, lintfree cloths. You can wipe excess off by going across the grain but *always make your final wipe in a given area with the grain* --or you are likely to have obvious streaks. Allow   the stain to dry for 24 hours.

• **Nongrain-raising (NGR) stains.** Like water stains, these produce an intense color when covered with a final top coat (i.e., varnish). Since NGR stains consist of a petroleum base with very little water, they do not cause the wood fibers to swell and raise. In general, NGR stains are not recommended for use with pine and other wide-grain woods; they are intended primarily for application on hardwoods with close grains such as oak and maple. NGR stains are basically an industrial product (commercial manufacturers like them because they are fast-drying) thus, it is doubtful that you'll be able to purchase one of these locally. If you do, however, make certain you read the manufacturer's instructions for use before using it.

• **Padding stains** aren't really stains at all in the strictest sense of the word. Rather, it is a method or system used mostly by professionals, for upgrading the looks of an old piece of furniture. Padding is not used on raw or bare wood. In simplest terms, it consists of applying a dry powdered color by means of a cheesecloth pad that has been soaked in either diluted shellac or lacquer. After such a padding treatment, a protective coat of shellac or varnish is usually applied.

The only way to learn about padding stains--how to use them, how they look--is to experiment with them on some old furniture of little value. Be advised that skillful use of a padding stain can eliminate the need for stripping and refinishing, in some cases.

• **Varnish and lacquer stains** have to be just about the ugliest finishes available. Actually colored finishes--i.e., paint--these add surface color but do not penetrate deep into the wood for permanent coloration. Avoid using them unless the wood on the piece you are working on is totally hopeless; that is, should be covered by paint.

Staining   tips

• You can create just about any color stain you may ever need by working with just three basic stains--maple, walnut and mahogany. Using these three in any one of an almost endless number or combinations, you can create stains to suit all periods and decor.

• For maximum tonal control with an oil stain, first apply a sealer coat to the bare wood. This will ensure the wood accepting the following stain evenly. The sealer coat I use is 3 lb.-cut shellac mixed one part to eight parts denatured alcohol. Apply this thin wash coat, then dry-sand it with 6/0 abrasive wrapped around a felt backup block. Dust off, wipe with a tack

rag and proceed with your stain. After the stain has dried, sand lightly once more with 8/0 paper, dust and go on to your topcoating steps.

• When working with an oil stain there is no need to panic if the stain dries too dark. Earlier we discussed what to do to lighten or darken a piece while the stain was still wet; here's what to do if you don't like the degree of darkness after the stain has dried. Saturate a 3/0 steel wool pad with turpentine and rub with the grain. Rub lightly to begin then, heavier if required. Finally, wipe with a clean rag. You can also lighten the tone somewhat with a light sanding with extra-fine abrasive wrapped around a block.

• A good home-brewed stain that is almost perfect for obtaining the "old pine" look so revered by lovers of things Country is one made from chewing tobacco. To make "tobacco stain", break up one plug of chewing tobacco into a one-quart jar. Add one pint of clear household ammonia; cover the jar tightly and set aside for one week. To spare your lungs, the day before using the stain, uncover the jar *outdoors* and leave it overnight to let the ammonia fumes escape.

To apply tobacco stain, wipe the surface with a damp cloth just before application to ensure even penetration. Place a piece of nylon stocking over the jar mouth to serve as a strainer and keep bits of tobacco from transferring from jar to your wiping cloth. Wipe the surplus stain off the wood surfaces with a clean rag and allow the piece to dry overnight. Next day, rub lightly with 3/0 steel wool before proceeding with your favorite finish.

Note: this stain dries lighter than it looks while still wet, but, usually two applications of tobacco stain are adequate. Also, remember, every stain gets slightly darker after a topcoat--even a so-called clear one--is applied.

PASTE WOOD FILLERS

As discussed earlier (in chapter two) not all woods require the use of a paste filler. But, those that do, such as walnut and oak, must be filled if a super-smooth finish is desired. Though paste fillers are available in colors, you are probably better advised to purchase the neutral filler and tint it yourself to suit the stain. This is my preferred method. You can make even the most subtle color change by using pigment from tubes, in addition to the stain.

Fillers come in cans and are of a consistency somewhat like that thick marshmallow which comes in a jar. The filler must be thinned to the consistency of heavy cream for use. To thin it, use turpentine; pour-in a small amount at a time, stirring constantly as you go, until you get the desired consistency. If it gets a bit too thin, add some boiled lineseed oil. Stir the mixture well so the paste is lumpfree.

Next, brush the filler on the workpiece using a short, stiff-bristled brush. To assure that all open pores are filled, the liquid is first stroked on with the grain then, worked across the grain. The filler should be allowed to set until it "flats out", i.e., loses its shine (about 20 to

BEFORE. Closeup of walnut surface after staining and before filling. Open pores which appear as light reflections would show through a clear finish as pock-mark holes, if left unfilled.

AFTER. Pores are filled as evidenced by flat lighting. The top coat can now be applied.

Often, minor scratches can be cosmetically treated with very little effort. Here, the scratch in this pine table's foot is minute–it just about breaks through the stained surface to the raw wood below. The repair materials? You guessed it–the cup of coffee and artists's paint brush.

A dab of strong black coffee renders this scratch just about invisible thus obviating the need for further treatment. Shoe polish can often be used for such minor repairs too.

30 minutes). When it flats out, using a rough-textured cloth such as burlap, start with an initial wipe across the grain, which helps to pack the pores. Finally, remove all traces of the filler from the surface using with-the-grain wipes. When satisfied that all filler has been removed, make a final wipe with a clean cloth. (Insurance against streaks). Set the piece aside to dry for 24 hours.

Note: Filler can be removed from carvings, finials, and the like by buffing with a stiff brush. Since rubbing-off paste wood filler can, be an arm-wearying task, it is important that you work only small areas at a time. If filler is allowed to dry completely on the surface , you will have to do some heavy scraping with a stiff aid--such as a scrap of plastic laminate--to get it off. Such an error could put you back to square one--stripping.

So make it your cardinal rule when using fillers to be patient. Work just a small surface at a time and do it right. In the next chapter we will discuss finishes. So read on to learn which finish appeals most to you.

5
CLEAR FINISHES

From this point on, patience both counts and pays. Although you now have the tiresome chores behind you (stripping, surface preparation, etc.) don't let your attention wander at this critical stage. How you handle the finishing from here on will determine whether or not your project will look professionally done--or amateurish.

SEALERS

More often than not, after a piece of wood has been stained, it should be sealed before applying the final finish. A sealer is applied because:

• As the name implies, to seal the surface. That is, prohibit further absorption of materials by the wood. A sealer also reduces the quantity of finishing materials you use.

• It provides a better surface for the finish coat to adhere to.

• A sealer preserves stain integrity. For example, it prevents an oil stain from bleeding into, and muddying, the clear finish coat. Over a water stain, a sealer preserves the quality of stain tone. Finally, a sealer will prevent certain woods (such as rosewood) from bleeding through the finish.

PRO TIP *If you use a pigmented wiping stain, read the label before brushing on a sealer; it may contain its own sealer. If it does, it will eliminate the need for an additional coat. Also check the label on the finish can if you are using one of the synthetics; some of these cannot be used over a shellac sealer.*

There are a number of sealers on the market and, since some of them do more than just seal wood, it might pay you to investigate and experiment with them. The best advice I can give is to read the label before buying, for two reasons: 1) so you know that you are buying the right product and, 2) so you know how to work with the stuff correctly.

Home brew sealer

Until you do fiddle with the commercial sealers, you can make your own by mixing together 3-lb. cut water-white shellac 1:1 with denatured alcohol. Pour the ingredients together then stir--do not shake--the liquid (or you will create excessive air bubbles that may show up in your finish).

Apply the sealer working quickly and evenly using a quality bristle brush. Shellac dries quickly and thinned shellac even faster. So you must work fast to avoid dried edges which would show. Usually, one coat of sealer is enough--unless you are using a commercial type that requires two coats. Let your home made sealer dry for at least four hours.

Next, sand the surfaces lightly with about a 6/0 abrasive paper wrapped around a felt block (see photo for authors stunt), thoroughly dust off the piece and wipe with a tack rag before continuing.

PRO TIP *Do as the professionals do and set aside a quality brush or two for shellac work only. After each use, swish the brush about in a can of denatured alcohol. Shake out the excess alcohol then hang the brush on a nail to dry. When the brush dries, the bristles will harden somewhat but, they will be ready for use immediately upon softening them against the palm of your hand.* <u>*NEVER WASH A SHELLAC BRUSH IN SOAP AND WATER.*</u>

You can save the cleaning alcohol by covering the can tightly. When the alcohol you use for cleaning brushes becomes thickened with shellac, strain it through cheesecloth and use it to seal out-of-sight spots such as chair bottoms or case backs.

TACK RAGS

Make it your work habit, when finishing, to dust off the surfaces thoroughly between all steps. After a swipe with your soft brush duster, use a tack rag. This is a saturated piece of soft cloth made so as to be permanently sticky by being treated with a nondrying form of varnish. They are available at paint and hardware stores for a very reasonable amount. Whether you buy or make your own tack rags, the method for use remains the same. And both can be used over and over if you take the time to store the tack rags in a tightly sealed container. If the rags become a bit too dry in the jar, i.e., seem to lose their tackiness, sprinkle in a few drops of water, re-cover the jar, and place it on a warm radiator.

To use a tack rag, wipe it across the surface as you would a conventional dust cloth. The only difference is that with a tack rag you can fold it for getting into corners to remove dirt and dust particles. But, you should always try to work with a tack cloth in a loose state, not folded tightly, like a pad.

Making your own tack rag

Select either a good grade of cheesecloth that has been washed several times or any other sound, lint-free cloth (such as a handkerchief or back panel from a man's shirt). Soak the cloth in tepid water then wring it out to remove excess water. Sprinkle with turpentine. Shake out the cloth loosely and dribble a fine stream of varnish on it. Make sure the cloth is fully spattered. Then fold all edges toward the center and twist the rag into a tight roll--this forces water out of the cloth. Open up the cloth, refold it and again wring as tightly as possible to ensure that the turpentine and varnish penetrate all the fibers.

Finally, shake it out and hang it up for a few minutes before using. The tack rag is right if it is soft and limp with just a trace of stickiness.

TYPES OF FINISHES

Though there are many products you can select from to finish your piece, the most common ones are listed below. Each type has its advantages and disadvantages, thus it is important that you give careful thought to the piece you are finishing to determine just which one is best for the task at hand. Basically, here is what you have to pick from:

- Wax

- Rubbed oil

- Tung oil

- Shellac

- Lacquer

- Varnish

- French polish

- Penetrating resins--which is really a finish system as well as a stain. These have already been discussed in Chapter 4.

You will be wise to only choose a finish if you are familiar with how it looks. You can always buy small quantities of the various products and experiment with them on scrap lumber. In fact, this is a sound route to better finishing knowledge. If you think you might like the looks of one of the following-described finishes, but aren't quite sure whether or not you have ever seen an example of it, visit a local furniture store or, better yet, cabinet shop to check out the various finishes firsthand. Here's a brief course on what you have to choose from:

For a shellac finish, the first coat is thinned 50 percent with denatured alcohol. Shellac must be applied quickly and with a brush saved for shellac use only. See text.

Wax Finish

Unless you have given it forethought, don't make the mistake of applying wax directly to bare wood. Because wax is absorbed deeply into raw wood it is just about impossible to remove it should you ever want to. The presence of wax, obviously, will prevent you from ever applying another finish in the future.

Thus, to obtain a natural waxed finish you must first apply a sealer coat, as spelled out earlier. When the first coat dries, sand it lightly with 6/0 abrasive paper wrapped around a soft-face backup block, dust off thoroughly and wipe carefully with a tack rag. Next, apply a second sealer coat. Let it dry for at least four hours then rub with 3/0 steel wool. Do this step carefully so that you do not form ridges due to uneven, or too much, fingertip pressure. When a wax finish is done this way, should you ever want another finish, you can remove the wax with turpentine and the sealer coat with a paint and varnish remover.

Applying a wax finish. Always select a high-quality paste wax that contains a high percentage of carnauba (hard) wax. One nationally known brand name is Butcher's Wax. Read the label directions for applying the wax that you bought. One method for applying wax is the steel wool pad method shown. The wax-impregnated steel wool pad makes a dandy tool for getting wax on evenly and obtaining a beautiful lustre.

Rub lightly as you start. As you continue to work you will develop a "feel" for the surface beneath your fingertips. At first, you will notice a slight resistance to your strokes. This diminishes as the rubbing continues. After a while, you should know almost instinctively when to stop rubbing the area. At any rate, do exercise some restraint at corners and in wide open flat spaces. On corners (outside edges) you can all too easily rub through the sealer coat, forcing wax into the wood's end grain. On flat areas too much rubbing in one spot causes dishing, I.E.; saucer-like scoops.

Let the applied wax set for about 15 to 20 minutes. Then buff with a clean, stiff-bristled brush such as the one shown in the photograph. Apply a second coat of wax. After buffing the second coat, however, bring the

Making your own wax pad

Carefully unroll the steel wool
pad and lay it out full length on your workbench.

Using a wooden spatula (clean paint stirrer being used here),
apply a generous amount of wax to wool at one end. Make
one complete fold and apply more wax as shown
Repeat step until pad is fully re-rolled and packed.

Wax pad ready to go to work. Author prefers
Butcher's Wax and buys it in large-size containers.
Smaller containers are also available. To wax, rub
pad parallel to the grain. You can feel when the
finish below your fingertips becomes smooth.
Allow wax to set several minutes then buff with a
stiff-bristled brush. Author's preferred tool shown
here is a scrub brush which was purchased for this
use only. Finally, if desired, you can buff the wax
finish to a lustre using a clean, lint-free rag.

wax to a lustrous shine by polishing with a soft, lint-free cloth.

PRO TIP *If you own a portable electric drill you can speed up the polishing step by using a lambswool bonnet chucked in your drill.*

Generally, at this time two coats of wax will be sufficient. From time to time the finish can be revivified by applying another coat of wax and buffing. Eventually, because of dirt buildup in the wax, you will have to remove all of the wax with turpentine and do the process all over again. For this reason, you might prefer to take a hard look at one of the eggshell or satin varnishes before racing ahead with wax, These finishes, as you will learn from the pages ahead, offer a handsome hand-rubbed look with a lot less work--and they are permanent.

Oil Finish

If you are not intimidated by a lot of hand rubbing, you might want to take a crack at applying this handsome finish. But, if you are not familiar with oil finishes you would be wise to first practice on a relatively small project. Though undeniably attractive, a rubbed-oil finish is a time-consuming one to apply. Another disadvantage is that such a finish has a tendency to attract dust. For this reason, an oil-finish periodically requires a repeat rubbing.

The standard mixture for an oil finish is two parts *boiled* linseed oil to one part turpentine. (Note: Some professional finishers prefer a 1:1 ratio.) It is very important to remember that you should never use *raw linseed oil* to achieve a rubbed oil finish because this oil literally never dries.

The boiled linseed oil mixture works best when it is heated. But, since the materials are flammable, never heat the solution directly over an open flame. The safest way is to use either an electric burner or to stand the can of mixture in a larger container which can be kept filled with hot water.

Though boiled linseed oil is often applied directly to raw wood, it is not uncommon to first stain the wood to help bring out the grain. If you opt for stain use a water stain that will leave the wood more porous than the oil types, which tend to fill the pores.

Make no mistake about it , you can count on long work sessions when you choose this finish. Read on and you'll see why:

• Apply a generous amount of the heated oil mixture to the surface and work it in with a clean, lint-free cloth. Continue applying oil and rubbing it in until the surface no longer absorbs oil. Discard rags as they become oversaturated.

• Next, using a polish cloth with a tight weave, buff the surface to develop a lustre. Continue buffing until a finger touched to the surface does not pick up any oil.

• Now, the clincher. The usual procedure for this finish is to repeat the above steps thusly:

  • Once every day for a week, then

  • Once a week for a month, then

  • Once a month for a year. And, finally,

  • Once or twice a year--every year thereafter.

Keep in mind that these coats of oil should not be rushed. Each coat must be thoroughly dry before applying the next one or the surface will become gummy. By now you have the gist of all this, and that is, in order to create a respectable looking oil finish you will have to apply somewhere between 12 and 20 coats of oil. So, if rubbing is your idea of sport, here's where you will get a healthy dose of it.

But, you can take heart from the fact that there are some commercial oil finishes available that let you cheat a bit on the rubbing. Several manufacturers offer oil finishes that go on in one coat--and spare you all that old-world romantic craftsmanship detailed here. One brand name that comes to mind that is particularly easy to work with and gives satisfying results is Antique Oil Finish made by Minwax.

Tung Oil

If you have never worked with tung oil you are in for a pleasant surprise: It is easy to use and gives a very handsome finish. The tough, durable finish is the good news. The bad news: The two major disadvantages (if you care to call them that) are the long drying time required between coats and the cost of tung oil--it's expensive.

Since tung oil usually darkens the wood to which it is applied, it is generally unnecessary to first apply a stain. To determine whether or not your piece should be stained, practice on a scrap of the same wood, or work an inconspicuous area (seat underside, for example). Try a sample area with stain and the adjacent area without. Then go with the method which is most pleasing to your eye.

As you should do with every product discussed in this book, take the time to read and understand the instructions on the label: The steps can and do vary from one maker to the next. In general you can count on new or stripped wood to absorb the oil more readily. In some cases it is even possible to apply the second coat within 30 minutes or so.

A tung oil finish is, literally, a hand finish--your bare hands are the best tool for applying it. Pour some of the oil into a wide-mouthed vessel (plastic bowl) and dip in both hands. Then rub the furniture's surface. The heat from your hands (friction) helps the oil become absorbed by the wood.

The usual practice is to let the first two coats dry thoroughly this can take up to 36 hours--before applying the third coat. Before it is applied, the surface should be buffed lightly with 3/0 steel wool to degloss it. Dust off the piece, wipe with a tack rag and rub on the third coat.

Three to five coats are the norm for a tung oil finish, depending upon the type of finish desired. Check the label to determine how many coats you should apply to get the look you want. The rule of thumb is: the more coats, the glossier the finish.

Shellac

For several reasons, shellac is a finish favored by beginning do-it-yourselfers: It is goodlooking; easy to master; inexpensive; fast-working; and, relatively durable. The biggest disadvantage is that shellac does not resist water, alcohol, and other chemicals (which will either discolor or soften it). For this reason shellac is not recommended for use on tabletops, bars, counters or other surfaces where exposure to such liquids is likely. However, when sufficient coats of shellac are properly applied, the finish is durable. Thus, it is often used on floors and other areas which are subject to heavy traffic and wear.

The word "cut" appears on every can of shellac and it probably confuses just about everyone. Here's what cut means: Suppose you buy a can of 3-lb. cut shellac. This label tells you that the can contains shellac dissolved at the rate of 3 lbs. per gallon of denatured alcohol. Actually, since you will almost always thin shellac yourself before using it, it doesn't make much difference which cut you buy. The thing to remember is--the lower the number the easier the shellac will be to work with. A l-lb. cut, for instance, will be a lot thinner thus dry considerably faster than, say, a 4-lb. cut. You would be wise to stick with one cut, thinning it as required for various chores. The chart shown lets you do just that no matter which cut you decide to use.

PRO TIP *When selecting a cut for a job, bear in mind that several thin coats of finish are far better than one or two thick ones. Floors and other surfaces subject to hard abuse can receive coats of thicker consistencies (i.e., 3 or 4-lb. cuts), you are well advised to stick with the thinner cuts for use on furniture: you will have better control thus obtain superior-looking finishes.*

Be aware that shellac has a very short shelf life; this means that you should only buy it in quantities that you will use during your planned work sessions. Leftovers, unless you are certain to use them in a couple of weeks, should be tossed out.

Applying Shellac Finish: It is ideal if you can work in a relatively warm room, at least 70° F, with low humidity. If you plan to do a lot of finishing it would make sense to purchase a dehumidifier to help control shop climate.

Shellac Thinning Chart			
DESIRED CUT	SHELLAC PURCHASED:		
	3-LB. CUT	4-LB. CUT	5 LB. CUT
1/2-lb. cut (wash coat)	1S, 4A*	1S, 5A	1S, 5A
1-lb. cut (good sealer coat)	3S, 4A	1S, 3A	1S, 2A
2-lb. cut (med. thin)	5S, 2A	4S, 3A	1S, 1A
3-lb. cut (typical)	Use from can	4S, 1A	2S, 1A
4-lb. cut (fairly thijck)	--------------	Use from can	4S, 1A
5-lb. cut (thick)	--------------	--------------	Use from can

*Key: S = shellac; A = denatured alcohol. Thus, for example, 1S, 4A means to mix one part shellac with four parts denatured alcohol.

Start by applying the shellac by the full brushloads in long, even strokes. Overlap following strokes slightly to produce a leveling effect and to minimize brush marks. Be aware from the start that shellac must be worked without lost motion. There's no stopping for a cup of coffee once you have started.

Once you apply shellac to an area, immediately level the liquid, then finish with brush strokes with the grain. Then immediately move on to the adjacent surface, while the initial edge is still wet. Once shellac has been exposed to the air, for even just a few minutes, it should not be touched again by your brush. At this stage, if you spot a sag or other flaw, let it be. It will take less effort to sand it later than it would to try to erase the spot while half wet/half dry. Your first coat will be dry in about 30 minutes.

When it is completely dry, give all surfaces a light sanding with 5/0 paper. Use an open-coat paper here because shellac has a tendency to clog sandpaper quickly. After sanding, dust thoroughly and wipe with a tack rag. Apply a second coat; when dry, repeat the sanding. You will not have to sand as much after the second coat because the wood fibres won't be standing. The usual practice is to apply from two to five coats in this manner. After the final coat wait two days then apply a coat of paste wax as spelled out earlier under Wax Finish.

Lacquer

Because it is particularly adaptable to production methods, lacquer is the finish choice of many furniture manufacturers. It is fast-drying--thus well-suited to spray application--and rather durable. For a number of reasons, it is probably the least desirable finish choice for many do-it-yourselfers--except for those with finishing experience, knowledge, and quality spray equipment and facilities.

The disadvantages:

• Lacquer cannot be applied over a mineral or spirit base. Thus oil stains cannot be used because the lacquer will lift the stain and muddy the finish.

• The finish will turn cloudy if exposed to water. Sweating drinking glasses, for example, will leave white rings in the finish.

• Because lacquer is so fast-drying it is just about impossible to brush it on without leaving brush marks. Though it is sold in two forms, one for brushing and another for spraying, many do-it-yourselfers will experience great difficulty in applying this finish.

Brushing on Lacquer : Since this liquid dries rapidly there is no margin for error. Do not waste any time once you start--this stuff is even tougher to handle than shellac. Once you start, continue until the entire surface has been coated. The lacquer solvent dries so rapidly that even the brush--if it has to be out of use for several minutes--should be kept suspended in lacquer, lest it harden during the work session.

If you opt to brush on lacquer, flow it on by the full brushload and stroke evenly and quickly with the grain. (As you do with shellac, only faster.) Ideally, the trailing edge of the just-applied lacquer will still be wet when you return the newly-loaded brush for the adjacent surface.

Lacquer dries hard rapidly so you will be able to lightly sand the first coat in about four hours. Dust it off, wipe with a tack rag and repeat the entire procedure to apply a second, third, and as many coats as you desire. Keep in mind that excessive sanding between coats of lacquer is not necessary. That is because each succeeding coat of lacquer will soften the preceding coat somewhat as it is applied.

Spraying lacquer: Though professional-quality spray equipment is available at reasonable cost from sources such as Sears, Roebuck, check out the low-cost equipment if your lacquer-spraying career will be a rather limited one. Be advised that spraying lacquer can be hazardous. If you decide to get into spray-painting, take the time to re-read that section of Chapter 1 that deals with the workplace. Through ventilation is a must in any room where painting or finishing is going on and special attention must be given to airflow in any room where spraying will take place. A large-diameter exhaust fan is required and all safety precautions must be taken to prevent even the remotest chance of fire or explosion caused by flames, smoking materials or sparking equipment. And, make certain you wear a respirator to filter the air that you breathe.

Spraying should always be done in a controlled

How to brush on varnish

1. Brush on liberal amount of varnish using with-the-grain brush strokes.

2. Then level the varnish with strokes across the grain.

To obtain a smooth surface, free of brushmarks, you must "tip off" the varnish. To do it, wipe the brush almost dry on can rim, then draw it across the surface—with the wood grain— and with the bristles at a 30° angle to the surface. Repeatedly wipe off the bristles so that the brush will pick up all excess varnish. The author does this by wiping the brush on either clean paper towels or a lint-free rag, *after each* pass over the surface.

The correct way to hold a varnish brush: Grip it in much the same manner as you grasp a pencil. Held this way the handle will contribute noticeably to balance, and wrist dexterity will be almost automatic. This is essential if you hope to achieve a smooth and level finish.

environment; the ideal room temperature is between 70° and 85° F.

Though I have read otherwise--usually in poorly conceived magazine articles and manuals by self-acclaimed, "experts" possessing little or no real experience--be advised that learning how to spray like a professional *does* take time and effort. You must first familiarize yourself with, and master, the equipment-- and then the materials. Make sure you practice with scrap before you ever point a spray gun at an expensive antique or piece of furniture that you've just built.

A lacquer finish can be waxed after the final coat has been allowed to dry a minimum of 48 hours. Apply the wax as described earlier under Wax Finish.

Varnish

I am frequently asked by students and amateur woodworkers which finish is the best choice for a home workshopper to work with. Without hesitation I advise varnish, for these reasons:

• Its comfortable-to-work-with drying time lets you work at a sane pace.

• It is not all that difficult to acquire craftsmanlike finishing skills with a brush.

• It is a clear, durable finish that resists water, alcohol and most other chemicals.
But, there are some drawbacks with varnish:

• Since it requires a fairly long time to set up, there is strong liklihood of a fair amount of dust settling on the surface. This, of course, increases the amount of time you will have to spend smoothing the piece later.

• Though it goes on clear, it does have a tendency to darken a finish somewhat.

Read the label when you select your varnish. For example, for a furniture project you *do not* want an exterior or spar varnish because these contain very little drier (so as not to dry out in the sun). Used indoors, a spar varnish would be a catastrophe.

When you purchase a varnish that you are not familiar with, take the time to read the instructions for using. In this high-tech era that we live in so many products change, so rapidly, you must be certain there are no exotic ingredients calling for some special skill, tool or application technique.

Finally, recognize the fact that when you work with varnish you must apply it to as dust-free a surface as possible. It is with this finish where your tack rags will do yeoman duty.

Happily, there are a couple of varnishes now on the market which set dustfree in the relatively short time of an hour or so. If at all possible select one of these for your project. McCloskey Heirloom Varnish is one brand that comes to mind (and is an excellent product to work with).

It is best to apply a sealer coat, as described earlier in this chapter, before applying varnish. Purists will scream "never use shellac under varnish because one finish shrinks as it ages and the other expands". This is true but, in all my finishing experience, I have never had a problem using varnish properly applied over a shellac sealer also properly applied. (I can't vouch for what the finish will look like 100 years from now, though).

If this concerns you, however, simply solve the problem by applying a sealer coat of varnish thinned four parts turps to one part varnish. Then proceed with the varnish finish.

To apply varnish, follow these step-at-a-time rules for sure success:

• Work in as dustfree an environment as possible.

• Use a tack rag, Q-tip, or whatever to get off every trace of dust before applying the first coat.

• Pour an amount of varnish, which you think you will use in your work session, from the varnish can into a clean vessel. Recap the varnish can immediately.

• Thin the first coat with turps using a 1:1 ratio.

• Apply varnish with a top quality natural bristle brush. Don't use this brush for anything but varnish.

• Brush the varnish on the surface, then work the brush at right angles to the original direction of application.

• Finally, "tip off" with an almost-dry brush held at a 30o angle to the work surface. This is a very important part of the varnish technique: tipping off actually removes excess varnish from the surface.

PRO TIP *I keep a pile of paper towels handy for tipping off. I make a single pass across the surface, wipe the brush on the varnish container rim, immediately make a wiping stroke on a paper towel, then return the brush to the worksurface to tip off the*

adjacent surface. If you keep the brush as varnish-free as possible, work quickly, and eliminate pools of varnish, your varnish will level and dry to look like a spray finish. You can be sure of it.

Ordinarily, one thinned coat followed by two coats of varnish full-strength, as it comes from the can, will suffice. You should lightly sand the surface between coats (see sandpaper chart for grits to use), dust off and always wipe with a tack rag. Allow the final coat to "cure" for several weeks before applying a paste wax, if you feel this is needed.

French   Polish

If you are refinishing a piece from the Sheraton or Chippendale era this is the logical finish to use because this is the look that prevailed at that time.

This is a far from easy finish to apply, and one that entails a high degree of risk. I have seen some allegedly experienced finishers foul up a piece with this finish. So, if you want the look, be prepared to pay the price in terms of hard work. Do take the time to practice on scrap wood--you will quickly learn why this is suggested.

To start, make yourself a pad for polishing. This should be about the size of a baseball and of totally lint-free cloths. To be safe, the materials you use should be washed several times to ensure all loose strands being removed. The pad should be of soft materials such as pantyhose or an old T-shirt. Dip this pad in boiled linseed oil (just as it comes from the can) until it is saturated. Next, wring out most of the oil. You are now ready to polish, a step-at-a time:

• Dip the wrung-out pad into a thin cut of shellac--1 lb. or less; then,

• Start rubbing the piece with a circular motion. *Important: Never start or stop the rubbing motion on the piece.*

• Always start a figure-8 motion off the piece and work onto it. Continue wiping--and wiping--until the cloth becomes dry or your arm tires.

• Then keep wiping and work your way toward an edge--and off it--without ever stopping the wiping motion until the pad is clear of the surface.

• Anytime the pad starts to get dry, work over to an edge and off so you can apply a few drops of linseed oil and a teaspoon of shellac to the pad. Then return to the wiping.

Now you can see, I am sure, why we advise the practice sessions. Also, as you have probably guessed by now, the trick in French polishing is in the application motion. The pad must never come to a halt on the surface or the area below it will become gummy and tacky. Continue applying the shellac as spelled out above until the desired degree of polish is reached. Then stop.

To remove the marks left by the pad's circular motion, wet a second, clean pad with denatured alcohol, and wring it near-dry. Use this damp pad by whisking it across the surface in *the direction of the grain.* Be aware that the alcohol in this pad is actually softening the shellac finish you've just applied so use it carefully.

OTHER FINISHES YOU SHOULD KNOW ABOUT

Polyurethane Varnishes

Often called "plastic" varnish, urethanes probably have a superior combination of durability, longevity, clarity and scuff resistance. A big plus in favor of using many urethanes is their short drying time which means, of course, less time for dust to accumulate on the surface.

In no event should a urethane varnish ever be applied over shellac or lacquer. If a sealer coat is desirable, thin the urethane (as described earlier under Varnish Finishes) and use it as the sealer. Apply urethane varnish in the same manner as resin varnish. To ensure first rate results, do read the instructions on the label.

Note: For most urethanes you can not simply recoat the finish a year or so later if you'd like to upgrade the finish for one reason or another. Urethanes, unlike their resin cousin, require the finish to be stripped and started anew.

Aerosol Sprays

Though these come in small containers, this material should also be used in a well-ventilated room. An aerosol is ideal for small jobs where brush marks are undesirable, but they are expensive to use on large jobs since most are priced in the $3 to $5 per can range.

The same basic principles for spraying with big equipment apply to spray-in-a-can:

• Build up a number of fine coats rather than applying one or two thick ones.

• Start and stop the spraying with the spray head pointed *off* the surface--never at it.

• Work with the can about 10-12 inches from the surface, and keep the can moving.

• Keep the spray head parallel to the surface as you spray. Don't swing your arm in an arc.

• As with other type finishes, sand lightly between coats, dust and wipe with a tack rag.

Stain and Finish in One

The newest finishing product on the market is the stain and polyurethane combination. With these you simply brush on the color of your choice and the job is done. If you want a slightly darker value you sand the piece, dust and wipe with a tack rag and apply another coat. It takes about 10-12 hours for a stain polyurethane to dry, I recommend at least one day between coats. The cleaning -solvent is turpentine.

These are okay for minor projects, perhaps a small kit you have assembled, or an incidental side piece, perhaps a stool, you just stripped. This finish does not have the authentic look of an oil stain and varnish finish--which I prefer--but it is far superior to the varnish stains of old. One brand that I have used and have had very satisfactory results with is ZAR Plus, Stain & Polyurethane in One. United Gilsonite Laboratories,, Scranton, Pa. makes it.

TAKING CARE OF YOUR TOOLS

As soon as you finish any work session, take the time to properly care for your tools, and clean up the work area (my Grandfather, who got me to love building and woodworking to begin with, admonished, "Clean up so you won't start tomorrow's work in today's dirt".) Good advice.

• Brushes used in shellac are cleaned in denatured alcohol only.

• Clean lacquer brushes in lacquer thinner only.

• Brushes used with varnish or urethane are cleaned by rinsing thoroughly in turps, washing out with soap and water, then rinsing with clear water.

• My preferred method for quality-brush storage is to hang them on a wall-mounted nail, bristle ends down. To keep bristles clear of shop dust, I wrap the bristles with wax paper or foil, held in place by a rubber band.

Fred Hale's Linseed Oil Finish for Mahogany

About 15 years ago, as the Editor of the Home and Shop Group for Popular Mechanics magazine, I visited the workshop of Fred Hale, in Winchester, VA, to photograph it for inclusion in a series of magazine articles that I originated for that magazine and titled, "Dream Workshops". Fred's woodworking projects, like his shop, were beautiful.

I admired the finish that he had put on a very fine piece of mahogany furniture, a careful replica of a colonial desk, Without hesitation, Fred offered to share his "secret" formula so that other woodworkers could know the joy of creating a linseed oil finish in much the same manner as the colonial craftsmen did. Here, then, just as he gave it to me, is his recipe:

1. Sandpaper all wood surfaces to a fine finish that no longer shows any sandpaper scratches. This should take you to 6/0 paper.
2. Make sure the raw wood is free of any oil stains or grease spots--don't even tolerate perspiration from your hands. If necessary, thoroughly wipe the surface with an alcohol-dampened rag before proceeding.
3. Apply one coat of the desired concentration of potasssium permangenate (burning agent). Application can be with a brush by wiping excess off on a cloth. Permit this to dry completely, then sand lightly with 8/0 or 9/0 paper to remove any raised wood fibres. If too much sanding cuts too deeply into the burned surface, a reapplication of the burning solution can be made since a second application will not significantly intensify the color. At this stage, any light spots can also be touched up with additional burning. Go over all surfaces with a very fine coated abrasive. At this stage, smoothness should be about what you expect on the finished product.
4. Using a brush, apply a 1:1 mixture of *raw* linseed oil and turpentine. Let this coat soak in for 48 hours; before proceeding, make certain the surface is dry, by wiping with a clean, lint-free cloth.
5. Apply *boiled* linseed oil (see the text on Boiled Linseed Oil Finish). The first coat can be applied by hand or brush; the second coat goes on with the help of 3/0 steel wool. The steel wool serves two purposes--it forces the oil deep into the pores where you want it and, it starts a polishing action on the surface. Work a small section at a time and make certain all visible traces are gone before moving on to the adjacent surface area.
6. Third and fourth coats are rubbed- in with steel wool and the excess is wiped off with a cloth. What is to be your final application should have the piece looking just about the way you want it to look when fully finished, but it will be slightly oily. Allow the last coat to dry for at least two days, then apply a "surface-curing" mixture comprised of 50 percent Japan Dry and 50 percent boiled linseed oil. Spread this thin solution on the surface using a lint-free cloth—and immediately wipe dry. In 24 hours the surface will be hard enough for the furniture to be put into service.

Burned mahogany will continue to darken over the years when finished with an oil finish. When it reaches a shade you would like to preserve, you can stop further aging by applying a good paste wax.

This is a beautiful finish and, if you decide to try your hand at it, you are advised to first practice on scrap mahogany so your furniture ,too, will look beautiful.

6
PAINT AND SPECIAL EFFECTS

Mistakenly, many of today's do-it-yourselfers think that all old pieces of furniture should be either stained or finished clear in order to appear authentic. Not so. In fact, the colonial (and earlier) craftsmen often painted furniture for a couple of reasons: a) to conceal less than attractive wood; b) to ensure the piece blending harmoniously in the room in which it would be used. Such was the case with many accessories, too. Typical examples that come to mind include the painted pieces created by the Shakers. There is also an abundance of painted work by Chippendale, Hepplewhite and other furniture masters.

Today with so much fast-grow wood on the market-- which, as a rule, does not take stain well and is often downright unattractive, you have every reason to wonder whether a well-applied coat of paint might not be the better choice. For that reason, in this chapter you will find step-by-step directions for getting the famous *HAMMERMARK* antique-paint finish.

Always give careful thought when deciding whether to paint or stain and varnish a certain piece of furniture. Very often an opaque color will enhance the piece's look. This is especially true when the piece is undistinguished looking--or, to put it bluntly--just plain homely. Generally, painting is the better choice if you intend to apply decals or do some stenciling ..

ENAMEL

Your should know that an enamel is just varnish with a pigment (color) added. Thus, recognize from the beginning that enamels are handled and applied using the same techniques as for the varnishes. But, there is one major difference you should be aware of: There is *less* margin for error, i.e., sloppy painting, with an enamel than there is with a clear finish. This is true because the goodlooking woodgrains which show through a clear finish won't be there to helpfully distract the viewer's eye when he looks at the painted piece. Thus, be advised that your job will draw raves only if the finish is applied with a professional touch. Read through this section completely to learn about enamels, re-read the Varnish Finish technqiue, then practice on scrap until you feel you have mastered enamels. You will be glad you took the time.

Enamels are available in gloss and semigloss finishes. The first type is often called the "wet look" because the high reflections obtained give the illusion of a wet or plastic surface. Such glossy surfaces were in vogue from after WWII to the mid-sixties. They are again considered to be "in" especially by those who prefer high-tech, Euro, and Art Deco furnishings. The fact that a good enamel will often let you build a project from easy-to-work with plywood, and then finish it to resemble plastic, doesn't hurt enamel's appeal either. A good example is the still popular, and functional, Parsons Table which can be easily built of plywood and finished with gloss or semigloss enamel, smoothed until the piece looks like it is of molded plastic.

Besides the oil-based enamels, latex and alkyd enamels are also available. Neither of these is worked exactly the same as an oil enamel, and neither gives the same results,. Oil enamels, like varnish, have a self-leveling action which will let you--with very little practice--create a relatively brush-free finish. Such results cannot be guaranteed with latex and alkyds.

There are also lacquer enamels--which are usually available in spray can form for consumer use. A typical spray lacquer is fairly easy to use and will give you a professional finish if applied skillfully. As mentioned earlier in this book, spray painting with small cans is the expensive way to go; however, in my opinion, these are a good and valid choice for small projects because 1) the job goes fast and, 2) there is practically no cleanup at job's end. You simply turn the can upside down, aim the nozzle at a waste receptacle or old newspapers, and spray until the nozzle is cleared. If the can is empty, toss it out.

When spraying enamels, do wear a respirator and

work with adequate ventilation. Check the instructions on the label before starting and, finally, remember that several light coats are better than one thick one.

Working With Enamels

If the piece you are going to paint is a hardwood with open pores, remember that those pores must be filled with paste wood filler before applying the first coat of paint. Paint *will not* fill the pores any more than stain or varnish will. So, to avoid those ugly pock marks in your finish, please refer to Paste Wood Fillers in Chapter 4.

When applying a paint finish to a softwood, it makes sense to first seal the wood before applying the undercoat. This is especially true if the wood contains any knots or sappy streaks. You can make up a sealer of 3-lb. cut shellac mixed 1:1 with denatured alcohol. Allow the sealer to dry at least four hours before sanding lightly with a 150-grit paper. Dust and wipe with a tack cloth before proceeding.

PRO TIP *Use only a top quality, superclean brush for applying enamels. Since you should always try to work with the widest-possible brush, you would be wise to set aside an assortment of different-width brushes for use with enamels only.*

To increase paint life, do as the professionals do after opening the can of paint: pour a small amount into a clean container such as a coffee can and reseal the original can. Refill your job can as needed. Using this method your paint will last longer because the paint in the original can will have minimal exposure to the air.

Undercoats

A paint undercoat serves several purposes:

• It provides a good transitional coat from raw wood to enamel; that is, a base for the enamel that follows.

• It makes it a lot easier to inspect for defects which should be repaired (i.e., filled and sanded) before the final finish goes on.

Be aware that some professionals avoid them, particularly on small projects, because of these disadvantages:

• It means you have to buy a second can of paint--of which only a small amount will be used.

• Undercoat comes in white only. This is a definite disadvantage when working with colors because it will affect (lighten) the intensity of the finish color.

The usual procedure to counter both faults are:

• If you will need a small amount of undercoat, make your own by thinning some of the finish enamel and using it as the first coat. Be careful not to over-thin the paint; figure that one part turpentine to two or three parts enamel is just about right. When this has dried, rub the surface with very fine steel wool, or use a liquid sander (my preferred method) to provide good "tooth" for the final, full-strength coat of paint.

• To minimize the lightening effect of a white undercoat on the finish coat, mix some of the finish

A spray paint in an aerosol can is a good method for obtaining a professional-looking finish on small and hard-to-paint projects, such as this wicker chair.

coat into the primer. Or you can squirt in some pigment of the same hue (color) from a tube. Either way, stir thoroughly before applying the undercoat.

Applying Enamel

Basically, there are two enameling systems. The first calls for a single appliction of paint after an undercoating. The other requires several coats of enamel and a bit of rubbing with a pumice paste. Which method to use is a matter of personal preference. However, be advised that the wide variety of good products available these days often prompts do-it-yourselfers to forgo the rubbing required by the second technique.

Here are the rules to keep in mind when working with an enamel:

• Work only a small area at a time. The size of the area to be worked should be determined by the speed that you are comfortable working at.

• Always use the widest-possible brush.

• Apply the enamel in one direction, then work the brush at an angle that is 90° to the paint application strokes. This step is to smooth out the enamel on the surface.

• Finally, tip off the surface just as you do for varnish. Keep the brush as dry as possible and pull it across the surface at an angle about 30° to the surface to lift off excess enamel.

PRO TIP *Since there is great risk of runs and sags in a gloss enamel finish, try to work with the surface to be* painted in a horizontal position. When that is impossible, make regular inspections of the just-applied paint--while there is still time to tip-off a sag--using a strong light held at an angle to the work.

The important point to remember about enamel is that once you start to apply it, you must keep moving. When working a large surface, for example, it is best if you work at a rate of speed--from initial paint application through tipping off--so that the lead edge of an area will lap the trailing edge of the previously painted area while the latter is not yet tacky. It is the only way you can avoid lap marks.

OTHER PAINTING TECHNIQUES

Through paint there are a number of "looks" you can create on wood furniture. Most of the methods are relatively simple, but all of them do require some practice to ensure successful results. Here are the finishes you are most likely to want to duplicate--in *HAMMERMARK'S* famous Step-At-A-Time format.

To antique a painted surface, a second color is applied over the painted surface, which has been sanded and dusted. Here, a wash-consistency black coat goes on.

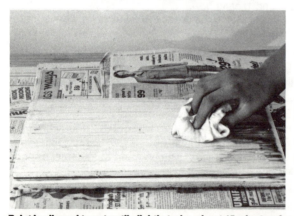

Paint is allowed to set until slightly tacky--about 15 minutes for an oil-based enamel, two to three minutes for latex, then wiped with a lint-free cloth. Paint is wiped so as to leave more paint in corners and in the spots that would not have been exposed to wear over the years.

Antique Paint Finish

This is the finish you want to use when you want to create a faithful replica of a museum piece or the like. Along with a number of other craftsmen, I have long had great feeling for Early American or Country Furniture. I never cease to marvel at what our forefathers were able to build from wood when they got to the new world. When you consider they started with a forest, and had no electricity, the results are awe-inspiring. And, for my money, no furniture made before or since quite comes up to the level of excellence set by the superb furniture makers in the short-lived Shaker sect. The colonial craftsmen as well as the Shakers frequently painted their furniture. A visit to any museum or restoration will bear that out.

Basically, you have two ways to obtain an antique-painted finish: 1) a kit, which is okay for a small project because of cost; 2) a paint from scratch job using the expertise we have developed over hundreds of finishing jobs.

Kit Antiquing

The most popular kits these days are those that contain latex products. With one of these kits you can finish a project in very little time and with relatively little effort. Both of these advantages are strong lures for many do-it-yourselfers.

The majority of these commercial kits are quick and easy two-step applications. Regardless of your brand choice make certain you read and follow the maker's instructions on the can. Techniques can and do vary from one maker to the next.

HAMMERMARK'S COUNTRY FINISH

For openers, be advised that antique painting is just about always done with two colors: A gray green (olive) over a blue; Federal blue over a black, and so on. The colors to use are up to you, or dictated by the original you may be copying. For purposes of clarity here we refer to the first color as base color and the following coat as the top color.

1. Completely sand the raw wood. In most cases on softwood, you don't have to go any finer than 120-grit. On hardwood, you can work up to 150-grit, if you think it is necessary. The trick is--*don't oversand;* remember, you want to create a somewhat rough antique looking finish. In fact, I generally do some rubbing with a steel-wire brush, at this stage, to cause striations in the softwood. When done with-the-grain and near an edge, this creates a very worn look--as though the piece had been exposed to weather over many years.
2. Dust off and wipe with a tack rag.
3. Apply a coat of stain to the entire piece. The stain to use is a matter of choice; its function is to make the wood look old when paint is rubbed off later, at edges, etc. Since that is the stain's only purpose, I usually select either a relatively dark pine or a light walnut stain for this task. Allow stain to dry overnight.
4. Next, pour some of both colors into separate

Closeup photo shows good example of antiquing with paint. This barber pole replica by author was painted with a base white coat, stripes and ball at top were then painted with blue and red paints which were wiped slightly to reveal some white below. To finish the antiquing, a gray enamel (wash coat) was applied and wiped.

An ebonized look is quickly achieved using black pigment from a tube. For larger projects, use black enamel , thinned with turpentine **as a stain.**

vessels. I make small "bowls" from aluminum foil because these can be thrown out at job's end. Also, if you plan to use additional colors, or white, gray and black, pour each into its own vessel. Finally, have available some of the stain so you can spatter with a toothbrush, if desired, to get instant aging.

5. Using either rags or brush, apply the base coat to the piece--work a small, logical area at a time.

6. Let paint rest for several minutes then, before it gets tacky, lay on the second color. If gray, white, black or other colors are also desired, apply them at this time, too. Then, carefully drag a lint-free clean rag across the surface to blend the colors. Note: A Turkish towel that has been prewashed to remove all loose threads, is perfect for this task. The object is to marry the colors to get a perfect blend--which does not look manmade. (See the color photograph on the cover of this book. Here, blue and green was subtly mixed.) *Take the time to practice and master this step, you'll be glad you did.*

7. While the top color is still wet, use an old toothbrush and either black paint or stain to spatter here and there but, *don't overdo it.* See photographs.

8. To ensure an aged look, you want to rub completely through the paint in several places to expose the wood below. You can either do it now ,while the paint is wet, using Turkish toweling or, wait until the paint has dried and rub selected edges carefully with a wad of 3/0 steel wool. The first technique requires more skill but is a lot less work than rubbing with steel wool thus, worth mastering.

9. If desired, you can thin some dark brown or black paint to a wash consistency using turps. Use this to simulate the look of years of accumulated dirt. Apply this wash to a small area at a time with either soft cloth or brush. Wait about five minutes, then wipe lightly with a clean, lint-free cloth. It is particularly desirable to leave some of this paint in crevices, corners, etc.--where dirt would have accumulated over the years if the piece were, in fact, an antique.

10. After the wash coat has dried the surfaces will have a flat look. This may or may not be desirable. If the former, the job is finished. But, if you want a slightly waxy-looking finish--you should never pick a glossy one for Country--apply one coat of a satin-finish varnish.

PRO TIP *Though you can use either latex or oil base paints to get a country finish. I urge you to stick with the latter. Oil base paints take considerably longer to dry and this gives the user far more control over mixing, blending etc. Additionally, if you are not satisfied with the paint's look after after you've worked the surface with Turkish towels and rags, you will still have time to wipe off the paint using a turpentine-soaked rag, and start anew. My advice is to master the oil paints before trying your hand with latex paint. The most desirable painted Country Finish, for my money, is obtained using eggshell or satin-finish oil-base paint. This choice also lets you skip step no. 10, above.*

EBONIZING

Stated simply, ebonizing is simply the technique of darkening wood with a black stain. The idea is to make the wood resemble ebony. Since a wood's grain reveals the species of wood as much as color does, there is little hope that the finished product will really look like ebony. In my opinion, a piece of eastern white pine stained black comes out looking like a piece of eastern white pine that has been stained black. Don't make the mistake of thinking that color alone can make one wood look like another: Except in certain instances (i.e., birch can be sometimes be substituted for cherry with success), it cannot. Thus, ebonizing should be done when black is wanted for the sake of black--not in an attempt to make a piece of wood look, like something that it is not.

MARBLEIZING (FAUX MARBRE--FAKE MARBLE)

Though not one of my favorite finishes, marbleizing in the 1980's is, admittedly, a very popular paint technique. For me, this technique is in the same class

FAUX MARBRE

Several colors of paint are dribbled onto a surface that has been painted with a ground coat. Your best bet is to choose colors by working from an actual sample of marble.

While paints are still wet but not yet tacky, they are patted with crumpled newspapers. Have plenty of clean newspapers on hand: Practice technique on scrap first.

as ebonizing--if it is done for the sheer fun of it, great. Executing the paint technique successfully--to deceive--does give a kind of guiltfree sense of accomplishment. I have also seen this used with great success by very skilled craftsmen and artists who use the deception to increase both aesthetic and intrinsic value of a piece of art.

My principle objection to this finish is that it is often used indiscriminately, resulting in a "kitchy" or corny look. One example that immediately springs to mind is a marbleized piano I once had the dubious pleasure of seeing. Somehow, a piano "carved" of fake marble seems insulting to one's taste. But, then, difference of opinion is what makes for horse races.

At any rate, there are times when this technique is perfectly valid. A marble top, for example, is often desirable as the top shelf of a colonial dry sink. When executed properly, this technqiue gives you that "marble" top at probably 1/20th of the cost of a bonafide one.

If you plan to marbleize, try to have on hand a piece of marble or, at the least, a color photograph of marble so that you can strive to simulate the look. Marbleizing left to nothing but one's own imagination can lead to disastrous results.

Marbleizing--a step at a time

1. In general, the idea is to apply a base or ground coat over an existing painted surface which has been sanded smooth. Depending upon the marble you are

Veining with an artist's brush provides a touch of realism. Take care not to overdo veining. Here, black paint is used.

trying to simulate, the base coat should be either a beige or creamy off-white.

2. When the ground coat has dried, other shades of color are poured on as shown in the photographs. The best way to pour is from small containers, which ensure greater control. Replenish them as needed. As you pour, there will be some tendency for abutting paints to bleed together somewhat; this is no cause for alarm. However, do take care to avoid building up large puddles of one or more colors.

3. Allow the paint to set about 15-20 minutes, then create the marbleized look using crumpled newspapers as shown. If you prefer, you can mix and marbleize the colors by placing a sheet of film plastic (such as Saran Wrap) over the wet paint, patting with a sponge, and then lifting the plastic straight up and off. That's all there is to it (but it does require practice).

WOOD GRAINING

Basically, this is a glazing technique used when the appearance of wood is desired on a painted surface. This is often used as the solution for refinishing trim in a room where it would require too much work and expense to rip out and replace the trim (or strip the wood in order to be able to stain and varnish it). It is also commonly used for wood-graining metal cabinets.

Though a simulated wood grain can never have the look of the real thing, some of the kits sold for this purpose let you do a surprisingly effective job. Generally, a beige ground coat is applied over a painted surface which has been sanded smooth or deglossed. When the ground has dried, a second darker color (glaze) is applied and carefully streaked using either a sponge or crumpled newspaper. The "grain" usually consists of nothing more than wavy streaks thus created. If you decide to make your own glaze you can do so by mixing varnish with burnt umber, raw sienna, ochre or a combination of these pigments. Some sampling is necessary before applying the glaze to a piece, as is some practice of the technique.

Simulated wood grain kits: As is recommended for all products discussed in this book, do take the time to read the manufacturer's instructions for the kit you buy. Some brands require three, rather than two, steps. Also, some makers include special tools that let you create more realistic looking wood-grain patterns. These are worth investigating.

SPATTERING

When done correctly, spattering will go a long way toward creditably "aging" a piece. The major temptation to avoid is overspattering. Because it is so easy to do, the temptation is a strong one: Resist it.

You can distress via spattering on both stained and painted pieces. In fact, many fine furniture manufacturers include this technique in their finishes. Take the time to visit a large furniture store and carefully check the finishes on the Colonial pieces.

Most professional finishers prefer using a toothbrush

Spattering quickly "ages" a surface. To do it, dip a toothbrush in paint, tap off excess and draw your index finger across the bristles as shown. Practice is an absolute must to avoid spattering paint globs onto the surface.

which is dipped in either black or burnt umber, thinned with turps. After excess paint is tapped from the bristles, the index finger is drawn across the bristles to create the spattering. Care must be taken to make certain that the brush is not overloaded or globs-- rather than a fine spray--will be released. Hold the toothbrush six to eight inches from the surface being spattered. Spattering should be allowed to dry completely before applying the final, clear finish.

LIMING OR PICKLING OAK

When a light natural look is preferred, pickling or liming is called for. Pickling is often desirable in a room with oak trim, moldings, etc. The idea of liming oak is to fill the pores with a white filler. There are commercial fillers

To lime or pickle a piece, the white paint is applied with a brush to fill the wood's (usually oak) open pores. After a short wait, the coating is rubbed off using with-the-grain strokes.

made for this: Firzite by Weldwood is one example. But you can do effective liming with a good-quality flat (white) oil paint.

The easiest method is to apply the paint using with-the-grain strokes. Next, the brush is worked at right angles to the application strokes to force the paint into the pores. After about 15 minutes, use a coarse, clean cloth to wipe all residue from the surface. Take care to avoid rubbing the filler from the pores.

The usual practice is to then apply several clear coats. This can be either shellac, varnish or lacquer.

SPACKLE-TEXTURE FINISH

Occasionally, a textured finish is desirable but, frequently, texturing on furniture is not permanent. The various materials used to create texture do not bond well with raw wood. You can create textures by using either sand paint or Spackle. Do not use these materials if the surface will be exposed to heavy wear, however. There are now several epoxy wood-patch materials sold which might let you do the job you have in mind. But, be advised that you generally will need

MILK PAINT

According to the supplier from whom we buy milk paint, skimmed cow's milk and buttermilk have been used as a vehicle and binder for paint for thousands of years. (Note: Our source for Milk Paint is listed in the Appendix.) Applying milk paint is no more difficult than with any other paint. However, be advised, once you apply this "stubborn" paint it is in the wood for good. Should you change your mind later, you will--in all liklihood--have to apply another paint color, you will not be able to strip the paint and stain the wood.

Here in captioned photographs is the way to work with milk paint:

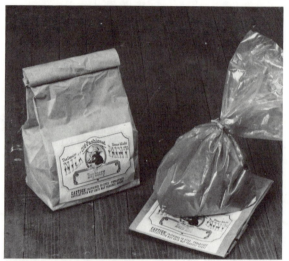

1. Milk paint is sold in bags like this in 6, 12 and 48 oz. quantities. It's available in six colors plus black and white.

3. Add an equal amount of water and mix thoroughly, at low speed, for 2-3 minutes. Paddle-type mixer for use in portable drill is perfect for this task. Add more water, if necessary, until satisfied with consistency.

4. Pour liquid through cheesecloth or nylon stocking into another clean container. This removes sludge, undissolved powder, etc.

the skills of either artist or craftsman so you can accomplish the desired texture in the relatively short work-time span permitted by most epoxies.

If you decide to try one of these products, do read and follow the instructions on the label.

DISTRESSING FURNITURE

This is commonly done to duplicate the look of a worn early American or Country piece. While there are those who despise the practice there are just as many who love the look of a carefully created antique reproduction. It's a matter of taste. If done correctly, distressing will enhance the looks of a Country piece that you have just built. The big error that many do-it-yourselfers make is to administer too large a dose of distressing. Here, less is definitely more; don't overdo it. The notion is to simulate aging and wear of furniture using manmade techniques. Thus, all is fair when it comes to duplicating the ravages of time.

By rapping with various types of hammer heads the piece will look like it has been bumped about.

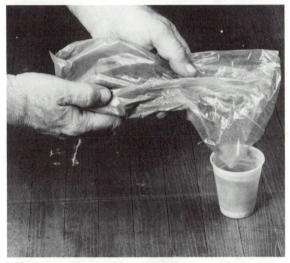

2. Measure out the powder, and pour it into a mixing vessel, such as a clean coffee can.

5. Working a relatively small area at a time, apply with a brush. If antiquing is desired, you can use a rag to rub off some paint along edges and other obvious wear spots.

6. If preferred, aging can be accomplished after paint has dried using 3/0 steel wool, as here. This method provides a little more control. Paint can be left as is or, if preferred, a coat of antique oil or tung oil can be applied to finish.

A propane torch fitted with a flame spreader is a quick, low-cost way to create "barn siding". Take care to avoid scorch marks caused by holding the flame in one spot too long.

Remove loose carbon by sanding with a medium grit abrasive. After thorough dusting, coat the piece with a shellac sealer. An eggshell (semigloss) varnish is a good choice for a topcoat.

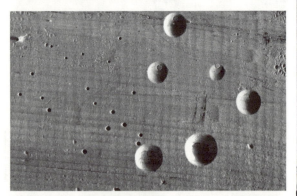

Quick effective distressing, exaggerated here to show effects, On the left are "wormholes" created with an awl; on righthand portion of wood indents that were made with a ball peen hammer.

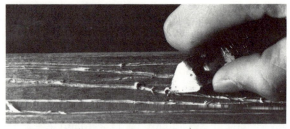

A striated look in wood moldings—often desired in picture frames—is accomplished using a punch-type opener.

Stabbbing judiciously with either icepick or awl will give the appearance of attack by worms. And, so on.

BURNING

This a low-cost way to simulate aged wood. Interestingly, the look is slightly different on each species of wood. The idea is to scorch the wood using a propane torch as shown in the photograph. It is advisable to attach a flame spreader to your torch so the heat won't be concentrated to a confined area. Keep the flame moving or the wood will burst into flame. The best way is to scorch lightly, then go back a second time if a darker look is wanted. If possible, for safety reasons, do your scorching outdoors. If you must do it in the shop, make sure you have a fire extinguisher handy should an emergency arise.

When satisfied with the degree of burning , sand with 4/0 abrasive and dust off. To finish, use a semigloss varnish. When done correctly, the wood closely resembles old barn siding.

STRIATING

This technique is often used to enhance a picture frame. Basically, striating is the etching of gouges in wood. One way to do it is with a punch-type can opener. If a two-tone color striation effect is desired, do the striating after the first color is applied. After sanding and dusting, the second color can be applied and wiped like a stain. The second color will be absorbed into and tint the scored areas.

7
DECORATIVE EFFECTS

Often, on finishing or refinishing projects it is the special effects that marks the difference between run-of-the-mill and exceptional results. For example, a plain wooden chair back, whether it is stained or painted, will generally be enhanced by adding a metallic powder (gold) stencil. Or a plain tabletop can be perked up visually with some judicious striping around its perimeter. Though the handsome results possible with many decorative effects imply a degree of difficulty, most techniques are relatively easy to master. Happily, a do-it-yourselfer with patience and common sense can handle all of them. If any of the techniques are new to you, try your hand at them in practice sessions until you feel comfortable working in that particular medium. You will find many of them just plain fun to do.

DECALS

Available at art, hobby and paint stores, decals are the quick way to a stencilled look. They are available in intricate designs, letters, flowers, and even in humorous patterns. These are generally used when additional decoration is desirable and stencilling is out of the question.

There is a marked difference in the quality of decals on the market. Some, when applied, appear to look like an actual painting. Others do not--no matter how hard you labor to apply them. Besides their usefulness on furniture, many find decals an excellent way to turn recyclable items such as coffee cans, cigar boxes, etc. into attractive, useful items.

If the decal is going onto a painted or varnished surface, make absolutely certain that it is dry before placing the transfer. To learn the easy steps for applying decals, see the captioned photos on the following page. Additionally, read the instructions, usually printed on the back side of every decal.

DECOUPAGE

In simplest terms, the idea of decoupage is to glue a print to a surface and then treat it with many coats of finish so that the print appears to be part of the surface--that is, painted on. Like decals, decoupage can be applied to almost any surface as long as the adhesive used is compatible with both the print and the surface.

The old-fashioned way to decoupage is still the least expensive because you can do it with materials you probably already have in your shop. Doing your own is easy but it does take a little more work than using one of the commercial decoupage kits.

At any rate, the print is applied to the surface after it has been painted, or stained. Then the coats of varnish go on. The steps for decoupage using the old-fashioned recipe are illustrated in the captioned photos in this chapter.

If preferred, you can use one of the synthetic finishes now available at arts and crafts shops. (instead of varnish). With some of these, such as polymer resin, the liquid is poured on and, when it dries it ends up looking like you have applied about 30 coats of the stuff. Though such kits do speed up the decoupage task, the finished work, in my opinion, looks like a speedy job. While I have had excellent results using the techniques shown on these pages, I haven't been too satisfied with the quick-job products. I just don't like the plastic look. But it is a matter of taste.

STRIPING

As can be seen in the photograph, striping is done with special short-handled brushes that feature extra-long bristles. On furniture the stripes are generally located near edges and they are applied rather modestly so as not to overwhelm the piece. Striping is probably the most difficult special effect to master. There is literally no margin for error because whatever you put on will be obvious. Thus, a crooked stripe, or a stripe of varying widths, will cause the finish to have the look of careless craftsmanship.

Since the striping does draw attention to itself, it should be put down with a degree of skill. The idea is to get the strip on with a uniform thickness and reasonably

The decal is placed in a tray of lukewarm water for about 15 minutes. Make certain the decal is left in the water the exact time specified by the decal maker or adhesive effectiveness my be reduced considerably.

Carefully position the decal in desired location and while holding the leading edge with one hand, withdraw the backing paper with the other hand.

Immediately rub the decal with a soft clean cloth to ensure a wrinkle-free surface. If any air bubbles exist, remove them by stroking the cloth to move bubbles over to an edge, and out. If this doesn't work, bubbles must be slit with a razor blade so that the entire decal lies flat.

straight. That's easier to say than do, however, Thus, it is obvious that striping skill can be achieved only through practice--usually lots of it.

Most stripers use the edge of the surface being striped as the guide on which to rest the fingers (see photo). But, if the stripe you want to place is too far from the edge, you can create a guide for your fingers to ride by clamping a straight piece of wood to the workpiece in the desired location. When positioning the guide strip, remember that the guide is for fingers-- not the brush--to ride against.

The best paint to use for striping is a slightly thinned enamel. Don't overthin or the watery paint will spread about the surface rather than remain a stripe. It is very important in striping that paint stays where it is put. Thus, paint should be thinned so that it flows effortlessly from the bristles, yet doesn't bleed,. Your safest bet is to experiment on scrap material of the same type as that which your finished project--which you intend to stripe--is made up of.

The most difficult part of the job is to maintain a reasonably uniform stripe width. Many amateurs have the tendency to leave very obvious signs of where each brushload of paint starts and stops. To minimize such obvious overlapping, rotate the brush slightly in your fingers as you near the end of a pass. Start the next brushload by overlapping the previously applied stripe to create the desired thickness, then drag the bristles along and continue as before.

But you might as well recognize the fact that any hand-striped line--unlike those made by machine--will have some waviness. Even those stripes applied by professionals on racing cars reveal a slight waviness when viewed close-up. The degree to which your lines waver will reflect your patience and practice.

GILDING

This is usually done on a textured surface such as a picture frame or on carved portions of furniture (i.e., chair back). Metallic paints are available at crafts and paint stores, usually in small glass bottles--because you only need a small quantity for most gilding jobs). You will find available a number of metal finishes including gold, silver and copper. Be advised that metallic paints must be stirred frequently during use because the metal particles quickly settle to the bottom of the container. Failure to stir the liquid regularly will result in an inferior job.

To create highlights by gilding, dip the paintbrush in the metallic paint and then wipe the bristles on either a paper towel or clean, lint-free cloth. Apply the metal paint to the surface using light, passing strokes. That is, use the technique that is commonly called dry-brushing. Keep in mind that a light application is the wiser choice. That way if any area looks under-gilded after it dries, the highlight can be intensified with a second pass. On the other hand, if the gilding is applied with a heavy hand, and too much is applied, the piece will either have to remain that way or once again be stripped to bare wood to permit a new start from scratch.

DECOUPAGE

1. Tear out the print that is to serve as artwork on your plaque. If you prefer straight edges, cut out the print using scissors instead of tearing.

2. If the print is from a newspaper or magazine, spray a quick-drying flat paint on the back side so that the type will not show through on the finished decoupage.

3. Hold the print in place and lightly mark its location. This aids placement later after glue has been applied. For this example, a piece of driftwood found at the shore is being used, as found, for the plaque.

4. After applying white glue to print back, locate it on the plaque using pencil lines made in Step 3. Place wax paper over the print and roll firmly to remove all air bubbles and ensure good adhesion.

5. Remove the wax paper and immediately wipe off all glue squeezeout using a water-dampened cloth.

6. For an antique look, apply some burnt umber pigment around the edge of the print,. The color should be darkest at the print edge and carefully blended into the picture and surrounding wood.

7. The finished plaque retains all the charm of weathered driftwood; the antiquing makes it look like the plaque is an old one. To achieve this look, eight coats of satin-finish varnish were applied, with a great deal of sanding between coats.

Striping takes practice in order to acquire a degree of skill. It also requires the use of striping brushes which are available in several sizes (foreground) at hobby and art supplies stores. The brush is held between the thumb and index finger and the third and fourth fingers ride the edge, which serves as a straightedge guide.

FLOCKING

The aim here is to create a surface that looks like felt. Though such a look is perfectly acceptable when properly used, as for the inner lining on a picture frame, resist the temptation to flock anything you can get your hands on. If you have any doubts as to whether or not a particular item should be flocked, pass it up. In my opinion, an unflocked piece of furniture has it over a flocked one--everytime.

Flocking is the application of thousands upon thousands of tiny fibers to a surface. Since several steps are involved, it is generally best to buy a flocking kit at the local arts and crafts store. Then take the time to read the directions that come with the kit.

In general, the procedure calls for sealing the surface to be flocked. Then a ground coat is applied and while it is still wet the flocking is blown onto the surface. After the recommended drying time the excess fibers are brushed and shaken off.

To spray flock on large projects use either a vacuum cleaner or power flock sprayer. On the small ones you can probably get by using a (clean) pump-type insecticide sprayer like the kind gardeners use to dust plants. Flocking materials are available in a great variety of colors and in a number of fibers including silk, cotton, wool and rayon. The last is the type used most often by do-it-yourselfers.

STENCILLING

If you intend to seriously pursue the art of furniture finishing, stencilling is one technique you will *have* to master. In no way can stencilling be considered a "gimmick" or "coverup" (as some of the other techniques are, in fact). Without question, it is a skill you must have in order to be able to do certain things. For example:

- When you have a handsome design on one piece of furniture that you'd like to duplicate on another piece. You will have to know how to stencil to do it.

- If you want to repeat the same design on a number of pieces, stencilling is the way to go.

- In addition to the logical reasons for possessing stencilling skills, you will find that it is also a very satisfying craft--once you have mastered the art.

To create a stencil design you can either draw upon your imagination or copy a design from a newspaper, magazine or child's book. There are many sources of inspiration for stencil designs: a visit to your local library can be most rewarding.

Basically, the idea is to create the desired design to a specific size on a piece of stencil paper (which is available at art supply stores). Generally, the drawing is first made on tracing paper and then transferred to the stencil paper via carbon paper. Once this is completed the stencil can be cut out and work on the project itself can commence.

STENCILLING WITH METALLIC POWDERS

1. Start by drawing or tracing the design onto a good-quality tracing paper.

2. With tracing paper backed up by cardboard, carefully cut out the design using a small-bladed utility knife.

3. When cutting out a stencil always analyze the design so that you are sure to leave connecting strips at critical points, such as between the pear and apple here (arrow).

4. The surface to be stencilled is given a coat of semigloss varnish. When it is tacky—usually 15 to 20 min.—carefully locate the stencil and press it into the tacky surface.

5. Rub the design into the varnish using a piece of velvet—pile side out. Velvet is dipped into pwder, tapped lightly on a piece of scrap then worked into the design with a light, circular rubbing motion. Use less powder at center of objects to create the illusion of roundness.

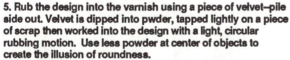

6. Next, carefully peel off the stencil. To avoid chance of loose particles of powder falling onto tacky varnish, first turn the board over and tap it.

7. When the varnish is thoroughly dry, wipe the surface with a water-dampened cloth to remove loose metal powder from surface. To finish, apply a coat of varnish, allow to dry, rub with 8/0 sandpaper, dust off, wipe with a tack rag and apply a final coat of varnish.

You must remember when doing a multicolor design that you will need a stencil for each color. This is especially true if you work with aerosol paints--rather than a stencil brush. In fact, in order to spray paint a multicolored stencil successfully, you will need a stencil sheet for each color, with a separate portion cut out for each color.

As has been suggested thoughout this book, a couple of practice sessions are recommended before stencilling a furniture project.

Metallic stencilling: Bronzing powder (which can be either bronze or gold) is frequently used in stencilling to create a look similar to that found on many Early American pieces such as the famous and beautiful Hitchcock chairs. The metal powders are applied so as to give a rounded look to objects like grapes, pears and other fruit. Although metallic powders are often most

63

often used with stencils to create the decorative effect just described, on occasion it is desirable to use either gold or bronze to highlight a painted stencil. In both cases, it is important that you learn to control any impulse you may have to keep dashing it on. Here, the designer's dictum, "less is more", is an absolute law.

Here, in our Step-At-A-Time style, is how to do metallic stencilling (refer to photo series):

1. Draw the desired pattern on tracing paper. Do *not* transfer it to stencil paper.

2. Using a razor-type knife, cut out the pattern. See photos.

3. Apply varnish to the area to be stained (whether the finish is painted or stained).

4. When the varnish gets to the tacky stage--usually 15 to 20 minutes under normal conditions--press the tracing-paper pattern in place. Note: if you do this too soon the wet varnish will destroy your pattern, thus making it impossible to rub on the metal particles. If it is done too late you won't have enough time to complete the design with absolute uniformity.

PRO TIP *By practicing on scrap you will soon be able to determine when the varnish is about right for pattern application. One test is to touch the surface lightly with your knuckles . If you sense a slight pull or resistance as you remove your knuckles from the surface, the varnish is just about right for metallic stencilling.*

5. Apply the bronzing powder using a small piece of velvet, pile side out. Dip the velvet into the powder then tap off all excess particles onto newspapers set to the side. Apply the particles to the tacky varnish by rubbing with a circular motion. Make certain more powder is deposited near the edges than at the center to create the desirable rounded look.

6. Once the design has been completed, carefully lift the stencil from the surface. Great care is emphasized here because you do not want any looose metal particles to fall from the tracing paper to the still-tacky surface, or they will be embedded there.

7. Set the piece aside to dry overnight.

8. Next day, turn the stencilled piece over and tap the back to remove obviously loose particles. Then wipe the piece with a water -dampened cloth. Allow to dry completely.

9. Apply a coat of varnish over the entire piece; set aside to dry for 24 hours.

10. To finish, rub the surface with 8/0 sandpaper, dust off, wipe with a tack rag and apply a final coat of eggshell (satin) varnish.

Painted stencils: Unlike designs created using powdered metals, a painted stencil is applied by using a pattern cut in stencil paper, and a stencil brush. Here's how:

1. Draw the pattern on tracing paper. When satisfied with your design, transfer it to stencil paper using carbon paper.

2. Affix the stencil to the dry surface using tape. The stencil must be absolutely flat with all edges flat on the surface.

3. Dip the stencil brush in the paint, then work out the

PAINTED STENCIL

The paint stencil is securely fastened to the work surface with masking tape and the design is applied by painting, stipple fashion, using a stencil brush. Note: It is important that all edges be flat or paint will bleed beneath stencil.

For additional decorative effect, outlining can be used after the paints have dried. To brush on decorative lines use an artist's brush and a complimentary color.

When all paints are completely dry, the piece can be protected with a final coat of varnish.

excess paint by tapping the bristles against scrap paper kept near the workpiece.

4. Apply paint to the stencil area with the brush held perpendicular to the surface and tap the paint on with a stipplelike movement. That is, move the brush up and down and apply the paint with a tapping motion.

5. Apply the design by working from the edge of the cutout toward the center. For a rounded look, apply less paint at the center of the cutout.

6. If working with spray paints, rather than stencil brush, try to do the stencilling with the work surface in the horizontal position, to avoid runs and sags.

7. If a second color is to be applied, allow the first one to dry thoroughly before proceeding. Though painted stencils can be achieved with enamels, they are--more often than not--generally done using latex paints. For a tough finish, the entire piece can then be coated with one or more applications of semigloss varnish.

Decorating a stencil: Often it is desriable to add details to a stencil (such as the brushed-on lines added to the bird stencil in the photos). This is generally accomplished using a fine-tip artist's brush and enamels. Use a dark paint to highlight light stencilled areas, and vice versa. Make certain that the color you choose for highlighting compliments the stencil colors. If in doubt about the color, highlight with a neutral (a shade of gray) or an earth tone (one of the browns or siennas). Stencil highlights should be added after the stencil has dried and before the first coat of varnish goes on.

GRAINING WITH COLORS

This is often done to enhance painted furniture of undistinguished shape or form. In other words, a piece whose looks can use a lift. Basically a two-step operation, graining consists of applying the dominant color, that is, base coat, and then a second coat of another hue, value or chroma. For example, the base coat might be a powder blue and the graining, or second coat, a midnight blue. Here's how:

1. Apply the first coat and allow it to dry.
2. Apply the second coat by brushing on to a small area at a time. Allow to set until not quite tacky--perhaps 15 minutes with an enamel, two to three minutes if working with a latex.

PRO TIP *Your best bet is to have on hand a piece of scrap. Do each step on the scrap piece first so you can be sure your timing is correct when you touch the project surface.*

3. To create the "grain", use either a piece of heavily textured cloth such as burlap or crumpled-up newspapers. Draw the "grainmaker" across the surface in one motion from end-to-end using a side-to-side motion. The idea is to create a somewhat (but not overdone) wavy patttern.
4. If desired, you can brush on a protective finish coat of varnish after the graining coat has dried. But it is not a must.

8

VENEERS, UNFINISHED FURNITURE, HARDWARE, AND METAL FURNITURE

Since it would be easy to write a book on the subject of veneers--and many have done just that--we will confine our discussion here to veneer basics. In other words, those points that most homeowners want to know about. Those who wish to pursue the art of veneering seriously are advised to acquire books dealing solely with the subject of veneers (many of the better craftsman supply mail-order houses carry such books in their catalogs). For the average home workshopper the trick is to know the difference between those repairs he can make and those which should be done by a professional cabinetmaker. What follows in this chapter is intended to help you make such decisions.

VENEER BASICS

For openers, know that a veneer is just an extra-thin slice of wood. Cut from log rounds, usually in 1/28" or thinner slices, veneer is used most often to provide an attractive finish over the lower grades of wood. For instance, it is often possible to build furniture of less expensive woods--or particleboard or fir plywood--then magically make the piece handsome by covering it with an elegant veneer.

Veneers are sold in a great variety of woods by a number of fine craftsman supply houses at relatively reasonable costs (see Appendix). In fact, if you must patch a veneer such suppliers are probably the only sources you will be able to turn to for matching exotic woods. Often, it is wise to send for a sample kit offered by a mail order house; the charge for such kits is nominal and then you will have on hand a large variety of veneers to choose from. In some cases, the sample may let you do the patching.

Applying Veneer

Though the following in no way should be construed as the last word in veneer application know-how, the steps are a reliable guide as to how veneer is worked with and applied.

It is not uncommon for a veneer slice to arrive warped and wavy. When it does, it is necessary to minimize disfigurement by moistening the veneer on both sides and then stacking it--under weight--to dry. Heavy, dry boards are perfect weights for this task and, if desired, clamps can also be used.

If you plan to use a water-based adhesive to affix the veneer, the clamped pieces should be ready to use in 4 to 6 hours. But, if you prefer working with a contact cement, as many professionals do, make certain that the veneer is absolutely dry (no moisture present) before applying the contact cement. This may call for 24 hours drying time. If you do opt for contact cement, try to use one of the types specially formulated for veneer work. This adhesive, too, is available from craftsman supply houses.

Regardless of which adhesive you choose, do take the time to read all use instructions on the label, then follow them to ensure satisfactory results. With contact cement, adhesive is applied to both surfaces and then permitted to dry for 20 minutes or so. The surfaces are ready for bonding when brown paper (from a bag) touched to the contact cement does not adhere. The patch-piece of veneer is then pressed into position and pressure is immediately appplied with a roller. *Caution:* When you use contact cement to affix a patch to a finished piece make certain the cement does not get on the finish or the latter will be severely damaged. It might pay you to mask off the finished surfaces.

Similarly, if any contact cement gets on the patch piece, it should be removed or the wood below it will not absorb the stain when it is applied. For ease of operation, many neophyte veneer repairers prefer using a water-based glue for a veneer patch. With this type of glue you have greater working time and there is considerably less chance of damage.

With a water glue the piece is immediately fitted in

QUICK AND EASY HARDWARE REJUVENATION

Sometimes the easiest tricks come to you quite by accident. After years of dipping and rubbing hardware to remove paint and revivify it, I learned the following stunt from Joe Provey, a longtime colleague in the magazine business, and friend. Joe told me that he discovered this trick while researching an extensive paint story that he was working on several years ago. Here is his recipe for "Boiled Brass":

You can safely clean layers of paint off brass door hardware, switch and receptacle covers by boiling them in water for about 10 minutes. After cooking, remove from boiling water, allow to cool and rub off the paint using a plastic mesh pot scrubber. Finish by polishing and, for operable hardware, add a few drops of light machine oil.

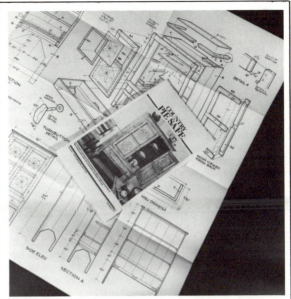

Many prefer to build their own furniture, rather than buy a kit, or furniture in the raw. For those woodworkers, HAMMERMARK ASSOCIATES offers complete furniture- building plans for a full line of Country Furniture--which blends with just about any decor. See Appendix for how to get a HAMMERMARK catalog.

This handsome colonial corner cabinet features a pair of glass doors above, with three generous shelves behind them for showing off a favorite collection. The authentic Pie Safe is a favorite with Country Furniture builders because it gives great storage, besides looking handsome. Both pieces are original designs by HAMMERMARK ASSOCIATES, which offers more than 20 additional original designs country and Early American furniture plans in its catalog.

place after applying the glue. Then wax paper is placed over the patch area and pressure is applied using either weights or clamps. The pressure must remain on the patched area until the glue has dried completely, which means leave the setup clamped overnight.

Repairing Veneers

Typical furniture problems and furniture care are discussed in Chapter 9. Here we will focus on the most common veneer problem--blistering. Generally, blisters are caused by water that has gotten beneath the surface and softened the glue there. Small blisters can often be repaired with an iron. To do it, the spot is covered with several layers of newspaper or a piece of terry cloth (to prevent scorching the wood). Then, the iron is held over the bad spot for several minutes. The iron should not be set too high--the "silk" setting is usually just about right. The idea here is for the iron's heat to soften the glue.

After several minutes, remove the iron and put weight on the sick spot overnight. You will find out next day when you remove the weight whether you will get off this easily. If the blister is a stubborn one, and pops up again, read on.

If the blister is small, say thumbnail size, you can try injecting glue into the bubble using a glue injector needle sold for this purpose. The first step is to soften the veneer (blister portion) by applying warm, moist towels. Then the needle is inserted into the bubble and thin glue is injected into the airspace. *Important:* Remember to use only a small amount of glue; too much and the blister will burst when you apply pressure. Withdraw the needle, cover the affected area with wax paper, add a wooden block, and clamp. Allow the piece to dry overnight in the clamped state.

Next day remove the block, and using fine sandpaper wrapped around a backup block, sand the patched area by rubbing with the grain.

When the blister is larger than thumbnail size you will probably have to slit the blister. The usual practice is to make an X slit in the blister using a razor blade. The four flaps are then carefully lifted up so that glue can be applied beneath. To prevent any chance of snapping off a flap, moisten the blister area thoroughly before slitting. Because of this step, make sure you use only a water-based glue.

When the blister is too large to be repaired using one of the abovementioned methods, or if the problem is a bad bruise or gouge, it will be necessary to cut out the damaged section and fix it with a veneer patch. Often, the toughest part of the job is finding a small piece of veneer that closely matches the original. The second toughest job is matching the stain and finish.

A veneer patch can be cut to any shape--frequently it is possible to use a particular shape in a certain location to help mask the patch's outline. When patching a plywood veneer, however, patches are often cut in the shape commonly called "boat patch", because the outline resembles a boat's hull. For more fussy work there are veneer patching tools which let you cut out damaged portions of veneer. The same tool is then used to cut the patching material from the new veneer so you are assured of a perfect fit.

If you do not own the veneer patch tool, start by cutting the patch from the new veneer. Then, hold the patch piece in place over the blister and trace its outline with a pointed pencil. Using a razor-sharp utility knife cut out the damage following the pencil line. Next, carefully scrape off glue and veneer fibers from the core's surface. Apply the glue and install the patch. Immediately wipe up any glue squeezeout, then cover with wax paper, a wooden block and clamp overnight.

Next day remove clamps and wood block and carefully sand the patch with fine sandpaper wrapped around a soft face backup block. Dust off and wipe with a tack rag.

When you stain the patched area, you might have to give it some special attention. For example, if the patch is on a finished piece the stain must be blended into the surrounding woodtones to eliminate any appreciable color contrast.

The above how-tos for patching and applying veneers are the most elemental basics: working with veneers requires a great deal more technique than we can present here. If the piece requiring patching is a valuable one, you might be well-advised to take it to a cabinet shop for a repair estimate. At the least, after reading the above material and talking with a professional who has looked at the damage, you will be in a better position to decide whether or not you are qualified to make the repair.

UNPAINTED/UNFINISHED FURNITURE

The first thing to realize when working with unfinished furniture is that most of the bargain-priced stuff is built of lower-quality woods. (The same is not the case for the majority of kits that I have seen, though.) However, some furniture-in-the-raw stores do boast a line of quality furniture. But, do watch out for pieces constructed of thin wood, or of wood comprised of glued-up blocks and pieces. The latter take stain poorly. On the other hand, if your needs are for a utility piece of furniture, e.g.; a storage cabinet for basement or garage, oftentimes the cheaper furniture, treated to a couple of coats of paint, is the smartest way to go.

This statement should not be interpreted as a criticism of all unpainted furniture. On the contrary, on a number of occasions I have found it more expedient--from both time and money points of view--to go with store-bought furniture rather than building from scratch. (Interesting side note: *HAMMERMARK ASSOCIATES*, the publisher of this book, is in the initial stages of developing a line of kits of the original Country Furniture designs in its plans series. These, the firm says, will be of top-quality wood.)

Many of the retail raw-furniture establishments that I have visited stock case goods in both pine and birch. The latter, in my opinion, is the better buy. Frequently, unpainted pine furniture is constructed using staple nails--and it is not uncommon for drawer bottoms to fall out when drawers are filled with weight, or for a carcase back panel to push out with little prompting. If you have brought home furniture of this quality, you are

Before : Typical four-drawer chest available in unpainted furniture stores. Wooden drawer knobs have been removed.

After : What some imagination and a few lengths of molding can do to change the look. Solid crown mold has been added to drawer fronts to create recessed panels; decorative hardware adds elegance. The piece was completed by surrounding the base with additional moldings. *(Photographs courtesy Western Wood Molding and Millwork Producers).*

well-advised to disassemble the piece and reassemble it using glue and screws before you ever start to apply your finish.

You needn't be a master craftsman to determine whether or not reassembling is called for. For openers, pull out and inspect the drawers; it is here that the degree of workmanship is quickly revealed. You can be sure that if the drawers are not carefully and well-assembled that the same workmanship went into the rest of the piece. Check drawer fit and and how they slide in their openings in the carcase, while you're at it.

If you do doubt the soundness of the piece it is probably worth taking the time to reassemble in stronger fashion. After all, you will spend a considerable amount of time and effort putting the finish on it; and, cheap or expensive, your finish-labor time will be the same. It would be disastrous, to say the least, to have to take the piece out of service several months later because it's falling apart.

"Jazzing Up" Unfinished Furniture

Though unfinished furniture is available in just about all styles--to suit almost any decor--it is safe to say that many pieces can be enhanced somewhat by the judicious application of moldings and hardware. Often, carefully chosen and applied moldings will elevate a chest with a cratelike appearance to the look of custom furniture. And the task requires very little effort. If you need help on this score, check out the literature available at your local lumberyard or home center. Several wood molding associations and a number of molding manufacturers offer pamphlets containing all sorts of ideas for working with moldings.

Very often, hardware used on unfinished furniture leaves a lot to be desired too. More often than not it is mundane in appearance and of inferior quality. As a result, much of it is cheap-looking and does little to enhance the piece. Frequently, by replacing run-of-the-mill hardware with more appropriate hardware from a quality manufacturer's line, it is possible to upgrade the look considerably.

The important thing to remember if you decide to fiddle around with moldings and hardware is to not overdo it. The temptation often is strong, and sometimes it becomes difficult to know when to stop adding. Once again, remember the designer's axiom--less is more.

Finishing Unfinished Furniture

Basically, of course, all the steps for finishing purchased raw furniture are the same as spelled out earlier for stains, varnishes, etc. The only point that you should be particularly concerned about is that you may run into some "wild grain" problems because of the species and quality in the furniture. The woods used most commonly for unpainted furniture are pine and fir. Both softwoods are produced by fast-growing coniferous trees. The problem of wild grain comes up because the softer summer rings absorb stain differently than the hard winter rings. In fact, the variation can be from a dark chocolate brown in one area to an almost white look on the abutting area.

Though this wild look seems to be present in all fir wood, that's not the case with the pines. Eastern white pine (which comes mostly from Pennsylvania) and some of the Idaho pines, for example, take stains evenly and as handsomely as you could want. Unfortunately, a great deal of unpainted furniture is constructed of southern or yellow pine--which take stain poorly.

The variation of grains can be diminished somewhat by using a sanding sealer before staining to equalize absorption. The sealer should be applied and sanded according to label instructions and then the stain can go on. Such sealers are available in clear and pigmented white. The former is used when stain will follow; the latter when the piece is to be painted.

HARDWARE

Often when restoring an old piece it is far more desirable to rejuvenate existing hardware rather than arbitrarily replacing it. In fact, many old pieces boast rare and, sometimes, valuable and frequently irreplaceable hardware that is superior to anything you might buy. Often, you will come across such a pleasant surprise. I did when I stripped the old table shown in Chapter 2. Here the knob was given a quick dunking in paint remover and, what I thought was wooden turned out to be exquisite solid brass. There was no way that this beauty would be replaced by a 20th century knob.

Though most old hardware is still usable after a good cleaning, you will occasionally come across a piece that

is not. But don't try to guess at a piece of hardware's usability until you have at least partially cleaned it.

Once the hardware is cleaned I like to protect it wtih a spray coating of lacquer (to prevent further rusting). However, sometimes the cleaning will reveal a metal finish that is pitted with an unattractive surface. In this event, keep in mind that any metal (except aluminum) that has been stripped bare and clean can be plated silver, copper, chrome, etc. Though this must be done by a professional electroplater, the cost may be more reasonable than you might suspect. For the nearest electroplater in your area look in the Yellow Pages under Metal Plating. The dealer will give you an estimate on the job you want done so you can make a

Next, rub the fixture with 3/0 steel wool. When i it's clean, neutralize the remover according to the instructions on can .

To clean up a heavily painted knob, tie hardware to a length of clothes hanger wire, then dip it in paint remover.

Finish the job by spraying the dry hardware with clear lacquer.

UNUSUAL HARDWARE IS EASIER TO FIND THAN YOU MIGHT IMAGINE

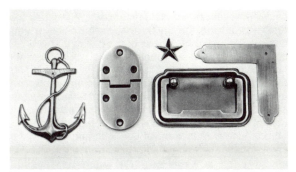

From left to right, decorative anchor, butler tray hinge, decorative star, and campaign furniture hardware--a pull and a decorative, protective corner.

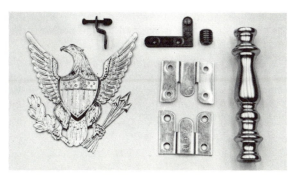

Decorative brass eagle, door frame glass holder, deep offset hinge, threaded insert, brass plated spindle.

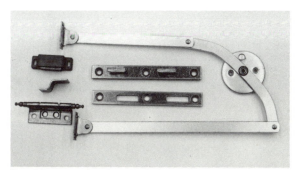

Special-purpose hardware includes such hard-to-find items as shallow magnetic catch, tabletop fastener, nonmortise lip hinge, bed hooks and cocktail cabinet fitting. See Appendix for sources for hard-to-find and exotic hardware.

sensible decision as to whether or not plating is worthwhile, or if the hardware should be replaced.

METAL FURNITURE

Now that vinyl (or plastic) furniture has replaced metal furniture as the number one choice for outdoor furniture, most of the metal furniture in use these days is indoors. The vinyl or plastic furniture, because it just about eliminates maintenance, is the most popular outdoor furniture sold these days. Most of it requires little more than an occasional wiping with a mild soapy detergent and rinsing. However, be aware that metal furniture used outdoors is exposed to the weather-- which takes its toll.

Indoors, decorators are leaning heavily on chrome furniture as accent pieces. The high-tech look, which persists to a degree, also brings into play flat black and glossy color finishes on metals. Such furniture accurately reflects the living style of the eighties; the furniture is easily cared for, freeing its owners to pursue interests other than taking care of furniture. In fact, the biggest favor you can do for your chrome furniture is to keep it waxed. A scratch on chrome opens the door for rust to begin. So, if a scratch does show up, clean away any wax buildup using turpentine, wipe the area dry, and rub the scratch lightly with 4/0 steel wool. Be careful not to enlarge the scratch: the idea of the steel wool is to remove any possible early rust accumulations. Next, wipe the spot with a clean cloth and apply a dab of lacquer (or clear nail polish) to the scratch itself. When dry, protect the area by reapplying a paste wax such as Butcher's.

Iron furniture--which is used both outdoors and indoors--is particularly susceptible to rust. Thus, any time you plan to paint or repaint iron furniture, begin the chore with a healthy rubbing session with a steel wire brush, steel wool, and sandpaper to remove all

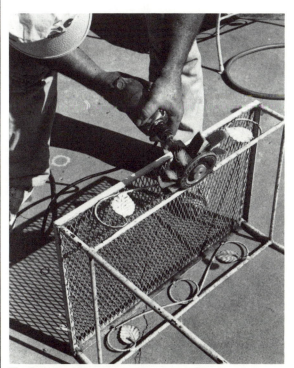

The first step when rejuvenating old metal furniture is to completely remove all loose particles of metal and rust, so the new paint will stay put. Here, Grind-O-Flex wheel is chucked in a portable drill to speed the chore. *Make certain you wear eye protection when doing work such as this.*

Metal surface is prime-painted--a gray metal primer was used here. Surface is then sanded lightly with very fine sandpaper wrapped around a felt backup block. Next, piece is dusted, wiped with a tack rag, then finish-coated.

loose particles of paint and rust. A stiff-bristled brush will do an adequate job but a wire wheel chucked in your portable electric drill will let you do the job a lot faster. Once all particles have been removed, sand the iron with a medium-fine sandpaper, dust off and apply a coat of rust-resistant metal primer paint. When this coat dries, brush on the finish coat in the color of your choice. But, make certain all of the paints that you use are intended for use on metals which will be exposed to the weather (exterior).

SAFETY NOTE: Make certain you wear eye protection whenever you grind and sand metal. If a fleck of metal should get into your eye it could cause irreparable eye damage. Don't take chances: wear eye protection.

It is a good idea to wax wrought iron furniture too. For one thing, the soft sheen improves furniture looks. For another, the wax gives good surface protection. Remember, outdoor furniture will be longer-lived when given a reasonable amount of care. For example, it makes sense to cover the furniture when it won't be in use for an extended period. Or, if practical, haul it into the garage for winter storage. Keep in mind that the more weather it is exposd to, the sooner it will need rejuvenation--by you.

PRO TIP *Outdoor furniture made of wood--such as redwood--should be sanded annually and treated with a clear wood preservative. Such maintenance will increase furniture life span and enhance looks by bringing out the wood grain.*

9
FURNITURE COSMETOLOGY

All furniture, whether new, antique, near-antique, or built from scratch in your basement workshop, should be given a reasonable amount of care in order to get the maximum pleasure from ownership, not to mention maximum life span. Thus, besides the aesthetics, it makes economic sense to take care of what you own.

A valid cause of poor furniture care, or neglect, is the confusion caused by the abundance of so-called "miracle" finishes. Though it is true that many of these new coatings are extra-durable and more resisistant to scratches, stains, and the like, remember that just about all finishes require some kind of care--and none of them thrives on abuse.

In no-nonsense language, here are the basic facts for good furniture maintenance.

DUSTING

Probably every homemaker, whether he or she cares to admit it, knows that all furniture should be dusted on a regular basis. The plain truth is that unless dust particles are removed periodically, they will eventually act as an abrasive and scratch the finish. Such surface scratches can be caused by sliding a hand or moving a doily across a dusty surface.

For this reason, on most finishes it is unwise to dust with a dry dust cloth. There are several fine commercial furniture cleaners available (one of my favorites is Guardsmen); in most cases, a small amount of the liquid is added to the dustcloth so dust will be picked up, instead of just moved around the surface. Dust cloths should be washed regularly and when you pick a furniture cleaner/polish (read next section) make certain you read the use directions before touching the stuff to your furniture.

Selecting a Wax or Polish

The type of finish on a piece of furniture--and the degree of its gloss--is the deciding factor when it comes to picking the wax or liquid polish to use. And,

be aware that no one polish is the best solution for *all* finishes. To be safe read the label carefully, *before buying*. When you have selected the product that you think is the best for the chore at hand, test it on an inconspicuous spot. If the results are satisfactory here you can take on the piece.

Which Polish To Use?

Here is a brief rundown on the most common household furniture finishes and the suggested methods of care for each:

• *Boiled oil finishes* must be cleaned periodically by washing with mineral spirits. After cleaning, wipe the surface with a clean, lint-free cloth. Then give the piece another application of boiled linseed oil (Chapter 5).

• *Flat varnish finish.* To preserve the flat, low-lustre look, use only a low-lustre wax on this finish. Apply wax to a small section at a time and immediately buff the area with a soft cloth. For more lustre,use paste wax.

• *Satin (eggshell) finish.* The best care here is with a cleaning polish or a cream wax that does not contain any silicone because this ingredient increases gloss. If the surface gets too glossy, remove the wax by wiping with a turpentine-dampened cloth. Then start building up wax again by applying wax according to instructions on the container.

• *High-gloss finish.* This can be maintained using either liquid polish or paste wax. Apply paste wax sparingly and rub vigorously to bring up the sheen.If liquid polish is preferred, pour the liquid onto the soft cloth--never directly onto the furniture--apply, let dry, then buff with a clean cloth.

• *Most paints*--generally an enamel on furniture--can be washed with a mild soap and water solution. Because of the glue lines, use water sparingly and try to keep it out of joints. Wash furniture only when necessary because over-washing with too strong a solution--will eventually bleach the color.

More About Washing Furniture

Beware of wax buildup on furniture surfaces. When you simply keep adding wax, eventually a masklike film is created that will hide the beauty of the wood grain. Wax buildup attracts and holds dust particles, and the resulting film can easily be streaked or smudged. In short, you can get to the point where wax can be detrimental rather than complementary, to the piece's good looks. When this happens, the old wax must be cleaned off with a careful washing. Then wax is reapplied and the system begins anew. There is no secret to washing furniture but, a fair measure of common sense is called for. A practical and easy-to-follow technique for washing furniture is suggested in the pamphlet, "Proper Care of Furniture Finishes", prepared by the National Paint and Coatings Association. Here's our Step-At-A-Time version of the association recommendations:

• Work only one small section at a time.

• Dip a cloth (such as toweling) into a sudsy solution of warm water and a good detergent, or soap flakes.

• Rinse the cloth often and, again, follow the wood grain with your wiping strokes.

• When it feels like all wax has been removed, make a final wipe with toweling dipped in clear water. Wring out the cloth well so you do not do not leave water puddles on the wood.

• When the furniture surfaces have dried, they are ready to be properly waxed or polished.

Furniture washing is as simple as that. However, there are a couple of points I'd like to add. The following observations are based upon experience gained from running my own custom furniture shop:

• You may find that more than one washing is needed to get down to the original surface. Don't yield to the temptation to do it in one step by using lots of water. It is better to wash twice, as spelled out above. .

• Stick with a soapy solution made with Ivory soap. It is mild and won't damage the original finish.

• It cannot be overemphasized that care should be taken to avoid getting excessive water in glue lines (joints). To be safe, wipe each area with a dry towel immediately after the clean water rinse-and-wipe.

Liquor Spots, White Rings and Other Annoying Blemishes

Chances are, at some point in time, some extremely careless act caused damage to a piece of your furniture. Though it is true that some damage cannot be repaired--except by completely redoing the piece--there are also problems that look worse than they really

are. In some cases, the offender can be completely removed; in others, it is actually a matter of toning down the spot so that it is less obvious. To do it, you must know the right methods.

Here is a checklist on the most common furniture problems and how to correct or minimize them:

• *Alcohol stains* include stains from medicines, perfumes, etc. as well as those made by spilled drinks. When any of these liquids (chemicals, really) are spilled on furniture, wipe up immediately and then vigorously rub the spot with the palm of your hand to get some natural oils into the wood. If handy, rub the spot with a cloth dampened slightly with an oil polish. To remove a dried-in alcohol stain make a thin paste of pumice or rottenstone and boiled linseed oil. Rub this paste in lightly working in the direction of the wood grain. Then use a clean cloth moistened with linseed oil to wipe off the paste. If necessary, repeat the rubbing. If not, polish the spot.

• *Bloom* is a misty or cloudy blemish on a varnish finish. It can be caused by a number of things including errors made during the finishing. Unfortunately, it is not always possible to remove bloom. Most professionals will recommend rubbing the spot with a soft cloth that has been dipped into a warm water and vinegar solution (three tablespoonfuls of vinegar to one qt. of water). This is followed by wiping with a clean, dry cloth, then a coat of top-quality furniture polish.

• *Heat marks*, the result of putting a heated vesel on a surface without using a pad, can be extra stubborn--and often impossible--to remove. About all you can do is try a little rubbing with a cloth that has been moistened slightly with either peppermint oil, camphor oil, or turpentine. If none does the job, try applying a thin paste mixture of rottenstone and boiled linseed oil. Rub lightly, wipe with a clean cloth, and then polish.

• *Burns* can sometimes be removed by rubbing vigorously with polish. If unsuccessful, try the same treatment detailed above for alcohol stains. If the burn is a deep one, that is, into the wood, you can figure that you will have to refinish the surface.

• *Scratches* frequently will disappear when coated with wax or polish. Be aware that a paste wax--such as Butcher's--can be color-tinted with a pigment. Generally, this is accomplished with burnt umber, but other tints can be used, if desirable. Or, you can try removing slight scratches with a wax stick (the type that looks like a crayon and is sold in lumberyards for use on wall paneling).

• *White rings and spots* are generally caused by moisture getting into the finish. More often than not, the objectionable spot is near the surface and relatively easy to remove. Try wiping the spot with a non-detergent household ammonia. Dab at the surface rather than rubbing it because too much rubbing (or too much ammonia) might harm the finish. Or, try placing a towel over the white ring and then applying a medium-warm, iron to heat the area and draw out the moisture. Don't let the iron get too hot--and don't keep

DO'S AND DON'TS OF FURNITURE CARE

Quality furniture--including those pieces that you refinish yourself--deserves attentive care. Follow these easy rules and your furniture will look better longer.

• **DO** heed the furniture manufacturer's instructions for care. Take the time to read the instructions that come with new furniture and then follow the suggestions.

• **DO** dust furniture regularly. When you do, make certain that you lift ash trays, lamps, and bric-a-brac (or eventually you will have permanently discolored areas).

• **DO** read the label on all furniture care products--oils, polishes, etc.-- before applying any of them to a furniture finish.

• **DO** rub with the wood grain when dusting, polishing, or waxing.

• **DO** use a pad under bowls or platters to prevent heat damage to your dining room table.

• **DO** use coasters, pads, or saucers under drinks, lamps, flower pots, and other containers for liquids.

• **DON'T** use self-polishing floor wax on furniture--it may soften the finish.

• **DON'T** expose furniture glue joints to water.

• **DON'T** use rubber mats or coasters unless their bottoms are felt-padded. (Some rubber compounds and vinyl films stain and soften certain furniture finishes.)

• **DON'T** wash furniture that is finished with boiled linseed oil.

It makes sense when dusting to add a couple of drops of furniture oil to your dust cloth. That way the rag will pick up particles instead of just pushing them about the surface. Dusting, like waxing or polishing, should be done in the direction of the wood grain. There are two reasons for this: you are less likely to scratch the surface by rubbing with the grain, and if you do make scratches, those made with the grain are less obvious than those made across the grain.

it on the surafce too long or you might create more damage than you are trying to get out. If these simpler methods don't work, rub the spot with a rottenstone paste mix as described under alcohol stains.

LAMINATED PLASTICS

Contrary to popular opinion, the high pressure plastic laminates are not impervious to all abuses humans can impose. Though the surface is a tough one, laminates should be given reasonable care. For example, don't slice vegetables or meats on the plastic--it is not intended for that--even when the surface is a photograph of a butcher block. A regular washing with a mild soap or detergent and water solution is recommended by laminate manufacturers. And now there is also available a liquid cleaner-wax formulated for use on laminates. It is easy to apply and it restores the surface lustre.

MARBLE

In general, marble should be given just about the same care as wood furniture. Coasters should be used under glasses, spills should be wiped up immediately, etc. Keep in mind that marble is just stone and, as such, it is porous. That is, because it can soak up liquids, it is subject to staining. In fact, it is particularly important that fruit juices containing citric acid and carbonated drinks be kept off marble because both can etch it. Marble should be washed frequently with lukewarm water and clean cloths. It is also suggested that once or twice a year a mild detergent should be added to the water in order to remove any residue accumulation. Scrub with a fiber brush, then rinse the surface and wipe with a clean dry cloth.

Do not wax white marble because it may take on a yellowish tone. If you want to polish the stone, apply putty paste (tin oxide), which can be bought at hardware stores. Apply it with a damp cloth rub for about one minute, then remove with a second, dampened cloth. Use a polishing stroke as you do . It might take some trial and error to develop the right "feel" for this. Start by rubbing with a consistency--but *not* too vigorously as you do with paste wax.

Removing stains from marble can be tricky and a lack of knowledge here can easily create problems of greater dimensions than the original stain you wanted to remove. Though some how-to manuals dispense advice for removing stains from marble, all my years experience as both carpenter and cabinetmaker prompt me to offer the wisdom that your best move would be to call in a marble finisher.

LEATHER

Genuine leather is used less and less these days in furniture--and with good reason. Many of the imitations look just as good, cost a great deal less and are easier to care for (not to mention valid ecological reasons). If you do have genuine leather on a piece of furniture, try to leave it alone for as long as possible. Dust it occasionally, and if its finish becomes dull, rub it with a good quality paste wax. *Never* use a liquid polish on leather.

10
PLASTIC LAMINATES AND SHEET ACRYLICS

Mention woodless furniture and you are likely to hear arguments for and against it. There are many who favor the use of plastics in furniture and probably an equal number who don't. The first group will quickly point out the advantages--to support their strong feeling for plastics. The anti-plastics people will scoff at the idea of a photograph finish on plastic--e.g.; a wood grain--ever coming near to replacing the real thing.

In my opinion both sides have a valid point. A wood grained plastic laminate never will duplicate the charm of real wood but, then, I don't believe the makers seriously intend to. For example, who would want a plastic-laminated grand piano? On the other hand, kitchen cabinet surfaces covered with a handsome plastic laminate make a lot of sense because they can be built of far less costly wood then the elegant hardwoods; and maintaining them is considerably simpler. In fact, they generally will retain their looks longer than wood because of the constant cleaning that is required on the various surfaces in this room.

Thus, whether or not to use a plastic laminate on a particular surface is largely a matter of personal taste--affected in great measure by common sense.

High-pressure plastic laminate (Formica and WilsonArt are two brand names) is not the only plastic used in furniture making. The second widely popular plastic is sheet acrylics. More commonly recognized by one of the registered trade names, Plexiglas, a sheet acrylic can be used to create furniture as well as for decorative objects, shelves, etc.

PLASTIC LAMINATES

The major advantage of covering furniture, countertops and the like with a high pressure laminate is the durability of the surface. Now available in a great variety of colors, textures and finishes from several manufacturers, some of the textured laminates are manufactured to such a high degree of realism that they easily pass for the authentic materials they imitate. For example, you can buy plastic laminate that not only looks but *feels* like hammered copper or pewter, slate and denim, among others. By the time this book is in print you can be sure that the major makers will have even more surprises in their lines.

Applying Laminates

No matter what surface you plan to laminate, make sure it is clean because contact cement will not adhere to a greasy or dirty surface. The contact cement is applied to both the plastic laminate (backside) and the core material--in thin even coats. When the cement has dried to the point that the surfaces can be touched with brown paper without sticking, the pieces are ready for bonding (laminating).

The laminate is then carefully placed over the stock and lowered onto it. Although a misplaced piece of laminate can, in fact, be removed and repositioned, it is a lot easier to take care when bonding it the first time--to avoid such a nuisance job. As soon as the two pieces are bonded together, pressure is applied using either a hammer and block of wood, as shown, or a roller (such as a rolling pin). Apply the pressure by working from the center toward the edges.

Laminates must then be trimmed using either hand (block plane, file) or power tools (router, carbide bits) or a combination of both. Final cleanup is with lacquer thinner--used sparingly near joints to avoid delamination--or benzine, and lots of rubbing. *Never* use a metal tool to clean a decorative laminate surface, you might damage it.

Working with plastic laminates is, indeed, a do-it-yourself task, provided you have the know-how, and a reasonable supply of tools. If you plan to tackle such chores in the future write to Formica Corporation (see Appendix for address) to see whether they still have available copies of their how-to booklet, "Do-it-Yourself With Formica". I am proud to say that I had the pleasure of creating and authoring this award winning how-to booklet for Formica, as well as taking the photographs which illustrate all the steps. I included in this book many professional tricks originated and used by my partner, John Gaynor, and me, when we ran our Custom Furniture and Kitchen Cabinet business. It has become the definitive book and has been referred to and used by do-it-yourself magazines and writers since it was published. But, by the time you read this it may be out of print. However, the key points for working with laminates are in this chapter.

Patching Laminates

Though surface problems with plastic laminate are generally minimal, there are two basic problems you should know the solutions for:

• **Blistering or bubbling.** This is usually caused by careless fabricating. Chances are the contact cement was either applied to a dirty surface, or that not enough of it was used. At any rate, the best method for correcting this situation is with an ordinary household electric iron set on "silk". Place several layers of newspapers over the offending spot and press the bubble. In most cases, the heat will soften the adhesive below and the bubble will disappear. Once you have heated the spot, keep weight on it until the laminate cools--or the bubble is apt to re-surface.

If ironing doesn't make the bubble lie flat, you may have to bore a small-diameter hole or two and hold the spot down with small brads. The brad heads can be carefully set ever so slightly below the surface and then covered with Seamfil (a patcher formulated for use expressly on plastic laminate).

• **Scratches, gouges, etc.** These are always the result of abusive treatment, that is, treatment which the plastic was never designed to withstand. For example, some people will cut vegetables and meat on a laminate countertop--despite warnings from the laminate makers to not cut on the plastic. A chopping block should always be used for these tasks.

If you do find a scratch in your countertop it can be hidden somewhat by filling with the product described above, Seamfil. The pastelike filler, which comes in a tube, is first worked into the crack; excess is then scraped off, using a scrap of plastic laminate and it is allowed to dry. The filler is available in a variety of colors, so it is possible to mix and match just about any color countertop. Seamfil is available from the same dealers who stock plastic laminates. Write to the manufacturer (see Appendix) if you have difficulty locating Seamfil in your area.

SHEET ACRYLICS

Though often chosen for use on furniture for no other reason than its good looks, sheet acrylics are frequently the most practical choice as well. For instance, if you want the look of a glass-topped table, but you don't want to use glass because of toddlers in the house, sheet acrylics will safely give the desired result. There are two drawbacks: the minor one is that

APPLYING PLASTIC LAMINATE

High-pressure laminate is bonded to core using contact cement on both surfaces, applied here with a nylon brush.

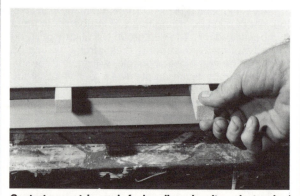

Contact cement is ready for bonding when it can be touched by brown paper without adhering to it. Laminate and core are kept separated using either kraft paper or 3/4" sq. sticks, as here. The sticks are pulled, one at a time, when you are satisfied with the alignment of laminate and core piece.

Immediately after bonding laminate to core, pressure must be applied. Do it with a hammer and clean block of wood.

acrylics tend to scratch rather easily. The bigger disadvantage is that acrylics are quite expensive. Especially when you get into the thicker stock.

Happily, the scratches can be removed without undue effort. Small, light scratches generally disappear when auto paste wax is applied to the surface and then buffed with a clean cloth. Deeper scratches require a

bit more effort, but even these can be made to disappear. The scratch is first given a light sanding with a very-fine sandpaper. This is followed by buffing with a very-fine compound formulated for use on sheet acrylics. Instructions for maintenance and care of sheet acrylics is available from the various manufacturers, generally through their retail establishments.

Next, trim the overhanging laminate using a router and carbide cutter. (A dull steel bit will result in a very rough cut; it pays to invest in the carbide cutter.)

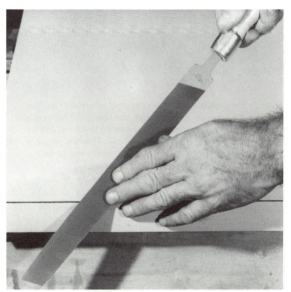

Lacking a power tool, trim the laminate overhang with a razor-sharp block plane; finally, finish -dress the edge using a smooth file. Work the file so it removes laminate on the downstroke only--*or you might cause a pullup at edge.*

To clean contact cement off decorative surface, use lacquer thinner (sparingly to avoid delamination) or benzine. Scrape solids off using a scrap of plastic laminate-*never a metal tool* (which might scratch the laminate).

Working with Sheet Acrylics

Working with sheet acrylics (Plexiglas) is fairly easy, once you know how. Keep in mind that plastics are not wood; thus, in general, you do not have the same margin for error when cutting or drilling. Exercise a fair amount of common sense when using the material; follow the manufacturer's instructions for use and you won't go wrong. Be aware that there are certain tools that make working with Plexiglas easier. For example, specially-shaped drill bits which bore very clean holes in plastic. The tools are available from the same retailer who sells sheet acrylics.

Sheet acrylics are available in smoked and clear as well as in colors so it is possible to choose materials that are perfectly compatible with the project at hand. There are also some patterns and textures such as pebble-finish, bottle glass, etc. to choose from.

If you cannot get complete instructions for working with sheet acrylics at your local dealer, write to Rohm and Haas Company (see Appendix for the address). This manufacturer's booklet is packed with solid how-to and the price is right--it's free. Besides the how-to, the booklet offers several Plexiglas projects. My advice is to acquire this pamphlet and read it through before putting drill or saw to a piece of Plexiglas.

Cut Plexiglas is by using a metal straightedge to guide a special scribing tool designed for use on sheet acrylics.

Saw and tool marks can be removed from edges by scraping with a sharp piece of metal (i.e., the back edge of a hacksaw blade.)

The scribed line is then positioned face-up over a 3/4" dowel (not visible in the photograph) and snapped by applying downward pressure on the narrower side.

Plexiglas can be decorated by spraying either with lacquer, enamels or oil-based paints (when the piece will be exposed to the outdoors). Spray painting provides the most even distribution of color and is easiest to do. The design is cut out of the protective paper, paint is applied, allowed to dry.
(Plexiglas photos courtesy Rohm and Haas)

11
PRO TIPS

In this book I have attempted to cover all the basic finishing and refinishing information that I think the average home workshopper must have at his fingertips--if he is to be successful at finishing and refinishing. My approach throughout the book is based--in large measure--on my experience teaching an adult education Basic Woodworking Course. In that class, frankly, I learned as much from my students (about what most folks want to learn about woodworking) as they learned from me (about woodworking and finishing techniques.)

The overwhelming majority of woodworking class students are always eager to learn tricks of the trade; the little ideas that make workshop tasks go quicker and become more fun to do. Though many of the time and energy saving ideas are second nature to the professional woodworker and finisher, rarely do you see such ideas in print. The realization of just how valuable such ideas would be for the beginner is what sparked the idea for the **HAMMERMARK** feature--**PRO TIP**--several of which are included in every **HAMMERMARK** furniture plan. You will also find them sprinkled throughout the pages of this book.

Here, then, are some of the best workshop tricks--all from the minds of professional woodworkers.

PRO TIP *SPEED UP REPAIRS*

Sappy streaks, common in some pines, must be removed before applying any finish materials. Use a pointed razor knife to carefully scrape out excess sap then, if necessary, clean area with a turpentine saturated cloth. (Ed. Note: Void must then be filled following one of the methods spelled out in this book. See Index, patching.)

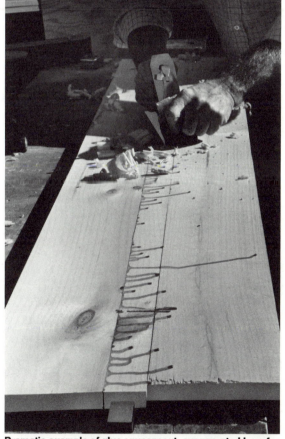

Dramatic example of glue squeezeout--exaggerated here for instructional purposes. To make glue easier to spot, author added blue chalk (from his chalkline reel). Because the glue was allowed to dry hard, it had to be removed using a jack plane with a razor-sharp iron.

Be aware that there is probably a piece of hardware made to solve just about any problem you will be confronted with when repairing and doing over furniture. This fastener, called Leveltite by its maker, is positioned to straddle an open joint then, when the screw is turned (right) the hardware forces the joint to close. Most craftsman supply houses (there are several listed in our Appendix) carry this and other exotic—but oft-needed hardware.

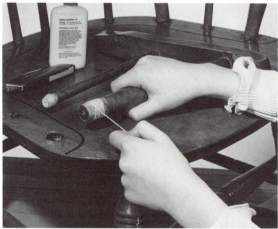

A chair spindle that pops out of its socket easily is caused by an enlarged large hole (mortise). Simply applying glue and reinstalling the spindle's tenon will not correct the problem. The surest fix is to tightly wrap string around the tenon, as shown here, apply glue and then reinsert the spindle. Keep parts under pressure (clamped) while the glue dries.

One of the toughest joints to clamp is the mitered corner. The next time you have to do one, try this trick to gain positive gripping for your C-clamp jaws: glue on small triangular blocks which will give solid purchase. After the clamps are removed carefully chip off the blocks using a razor-sharp chisel.

PRO TIP *SANDING STUNTS*

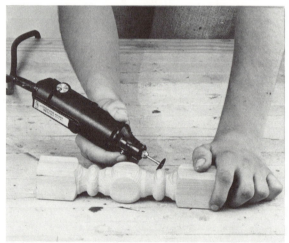

A quick and easy way to sand small spindles, beads, coves and the like is with this small tool, chucked with a small-dia. sanding disc. Several manufacturers now produce such tools, the one shown is the Dremel Moto Tool by Emerson Electric.

For bigger scroll shapes use a sanding drum in your electric drill. These are available at your local hardware store in a number of diameters. The sanding sleeves are inexpensive yet, ruggedly built to do a considerable amount of sanding.

Several manufacturers now make sanding blocks which come with their backup "block" built in. The one shown, Quicksand by Zynolyte, has abrasive grit applied on all four sides of a soft material. To clean the abrasive, simply hold it under running water and wring it out. The hand sanders are one of the author's favorite sanding tools for smoothing items while still mounted on the wood lathe.

PRO TIP *FINISHING EXPERTISE*

Whenever possible, apply a finish to a surface in the horizontal position to avoid sags and runs. Here, a one-step stain/urethane finish is being applied to a table top.

A very quick–as well as very easy–way to stain is with a spray type, such as this one. Big advantage: time saved plus minimal fuss and dirt. Drawbacks: stain cannot be custom mixed to a desired color and, since stain in a spray can is more expensive, unless budget doesn't matter, save it for your smaller staining tasks.

A quick way to "antique" a stained piece is with pigment applied with a rag, as shown here. Generally, burnt umber is the best pigment to use. Make sure pigment is blended into the stain–you do not want a sudden change in tones.

An easy way to pick a foreign object, lint, etc., from a just-varnished surface is with a small artist's brush. Keep several sizes on hand just for this purpose.

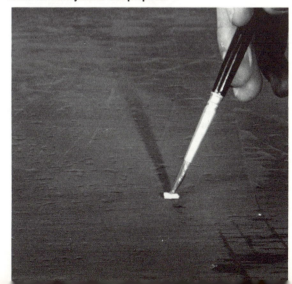

Budget-priced paint shop. To spray small objects all you need is a board mounted on lazy Susan hardware and a low-cost photographer's lamp with a 500 watt bulb. As you spray the piece you can rotate the lazy Susan to watch for holidays, streaks and sags. The light will give the most help if aimed to glance off at about 45°.

PRO TIP *CLEANING BRUSHES*

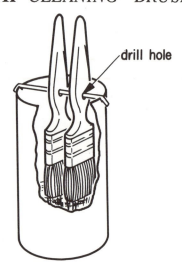

drill hole

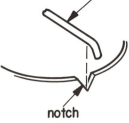

clothes hanger wire

notch

To keep brushes soft, should your paint or varnish session be interrupted, simply suspend them in the appropriate solvent for the paint you're using. You can fashion this setup quickly, all you need is a clean coffee can, a wire hanger and a drill for boring the correct-size holes through the brush handles.

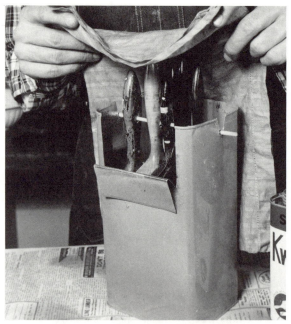

To make paint-hardened brushes soft once again, you must suspend them in a brush cleaner for a period of time; overnight at the least and often for a 24 hours. A large can like the one shown lets you can clean several brushes at a time.

Use an old fork to open up the bristles.

The best way to store a clean and dry brush? Wrap it in paper and secure wrapping with a rubber band.

PRO TIP *IDEAS FOR WOODWORKERS*

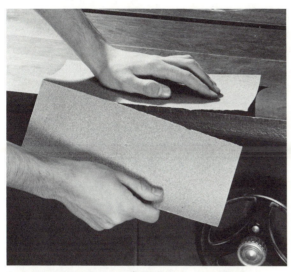

Easiest and fastest way to get full sheets of sandpaper to usable sander-size sheets: fold a sharp crease at the point you want to do the cutting; hold the crease over the sharp metal edge of your table saw and tear with one motion.

Most cabinetmakers use a half-size template (or pattern) rather than making a full–size one. Use 1/4" thick hardboard or plywood to make your patterns, and draw a n accurate centerline, as here.

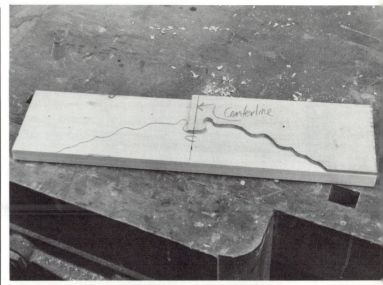

After drawing-in the first half of the pattern, flop the pattern, align the centerline and edges carefully, and use your pencil to mark the other half. of the workpiece.

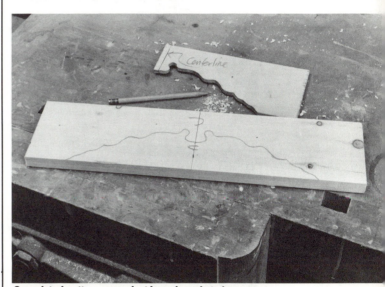

Completed pattern on project board, ready to be cut out.

GREAT PLANS
COUNTRY FURNITURE AT ITS VERY BEST

Shown on this page are several examples of the superb Country furniture designs offered by **HAMMERMARK ASSOCIATES.** We believe these are the best-available Country furniture plans for home workshoppers. All designs are originals--some are exact replicas of antiques, while others are from the craftsman's creative mind-- but, designed using authentic elements only The plans include instructions and drawings to make the building easier and more fun. All plans include full instructions for duplicating the finish, used on the prototype pieces.

Four beautiful pieces from the HAMMERMARK COLLECTION--and there are more than 20 additional designs to choose from.

CORNER CABINET
No. 821

18th CENTURY PIE SAFE
No. 8417

OAK ICEBOX
No. 836

86

SHAKER DRESSER
No. 8733

CATALOG AVAILABLE

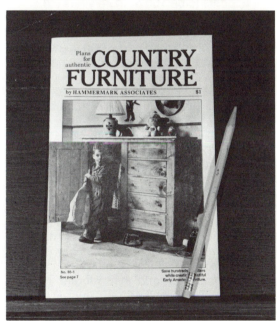

Send for the Hammermark catalog which lists all available products--most of which are carried by Hammermark only.

The catalog is priced at $1.-which is refunded with your first order.

Write to: HAMMERMARK ASSOCIATES, P.O. BOX 201-FB, FLORAL PARK, N.Y. 11002.

Specialty items for home workshoppers

CRAFTSMAN'S WAX FINISH
No. 8735P

5 POSTERS FOR ANTIQUING
No. 8522P

87

GLOSSARY

Abrasive: a product used for smoothing, such as sandpaper, steel wool, pumice, and rottenstone.

Acrylic: a plastic resin that is used in latex and in some fast-drying enamels. Also, sheet acrylics, such as Plexiglas and Lucite.

Adhesion: the characteristic of a paint to adhere to the previously-applied coat.

Alkyd: a synthetic resin made form chemicals. Most paints today (those which are thinned with solvents) contain alkyd resins.

Alligatoring: a term used to describe a deteriorating coat of paint. The descriptive word refers to a finish with cracks that resemble an alligator's hide.

Aniline dyes: those made from coal tar or coat tar derivatives.

Antiquing: a furniture finishing system to simulate aging through use of excessive wear spots and color combinations.

Base coat: the first coat of color (does not include sealers or sanding sealers); also the base color applied when glazing (as with an antiquing kit).

Binder: that part of a paint medium which holds the pigment in coherent film when the paint dries. Binder can be oil, resin or size, and is not volatile.

Bleach: to restore wood or make it lighter through use of chemicals. Often done with oxalic acid crystals or powders.

Bleeding: discoloration from beneath that shows through the finish coat. It can often be controlled through the use of sealers.

Bloom: imperfection in a finish. Generally caused by foreign deposits in the finish while it is still wet.

Body (viscosity): thickness, or consistency of a fluid.

Boiled linseed oil: has chemical driers added at the factory. Never try to boil either boiled or raw linseed oil. Boiled linseed oil, unlike raw linseed oil, will eventually dry.

Chinawood oil: see Tung oil.

Close-grain wood: has pores that are not revealed when finish dries (examples are birch, cherry, maple).

Country paint: a paint finish carefully applied so it appears to be 100 or more years old.

Denatured alcohol: shellac solvent.

Drier: chemical compounds for hastening the drying time of enamels. Use with caution, and only in amounts specified on the paint can label.

Enamel: usually glossy or semiglossy finish because the paint contains a high percentage of varnish.

Epoxy: latter-day type of synthetic resin that boasts a high resistance to most chemicals. Some versions require adding a catalyst to form the film.

Feathering: blending the edges of one area of paint into the adjacent area so as not to show brush lap marks. Also, feathering an antique tone, e.g., burnt umber, from the corner of a piece out into adjacent open areas of a piece.

Filler, paste wood: material must be thinned to cream consistency and then rubbed into the pores of open-grain woods.

Flat finish: dries with a rubbedlike look. No sheen.

French polish: a linseed oil/shellac finish applied using a time-proven method. Produces a handsome but not too durable finish.

Glazing: an antiquing technique whereby a second, semiopaque color is brushed on (over a color) and then wiped off.

Glossy finish: a very high shine, usually in enamels, high-gloss varnishes and certain paint lacquers. Often called the wet look.

Graining: simulation of wood grain using a base color coat followed by a coat of another color which is then "grained" using newspaper, rags, combs, or other instruments.

Hardwood: wood from deciduous trees (e.g., broadleafed).

Knot: portion of a limb or branch that is surrounded by subsequent growth of the tree.

Lacquer: a fast-drying finishing material. A poor choice for beginning finishers.

Latex: dispersion emulsion of rubber or rubber-like resin in water.

Milk paint: paint produced to give an "old" look; that is, a flat, grainey appearance. In colonial times, skimmed cow's milk and buttermilk were used as the vehicle and binder.

Mineral spirits: petroleum base thinner.

NGR stain: nongrain- raising stain contains little or no water thus doesn't swell wood fibers or cause grain to stand.

Oil stain: dye in oil or oleoresinous base. Pigmented wiping ·stains are also often referred to as oil stains.

Open-grain wood: such as walnut, oak, and chestnut, has conspicuous pores. Open-grain woods must be filled with paste wood fillers before finishing because most finishes will not bridge the pores.

Orange peel: rough, textured finish caused by improper balance of solvent and finish when spraying. So-named because the finish has the look and feel of orange peel.

Paste wood filler: see filler, paste wood.

Patina: on wood, color and texture added to a surface by time weathering and other factors (such as rubbing and waxing). On copper, it is the greenish coating called verdigris.

Penetrating finish: a finish that is formulated to penetrate deep into wood, leaving little or no finish on the surface to be wiped off.

Pigment: fine-ground particles which must be stirred into oils varnishes, lacquers, etc. Pigments are added to the vehicle to impart color and hiding power.

Pumice: finely-ground stone used with oil to achieve a satin-like finish on furniture.

Refinisher: a chemical product of the 1980's that allows revivification of the finish on a piece of furniture without stripping the old finish, and destroying partina.

Resin: material which forms film for finish. *Also see Binder.*

Retarder: chemcial for slowing down paint drying time.

Rottenstone: very fine limestone powder used after pumice, if a high gloss is desirable.

Rubbed finish: a finish of ultimate smoothness obtained by rubbing varnish with pumice and oil, or with very-fine waterproof sandpaper.

Rubbing varnish: most varnishes today will take a rubbing. Generally rubbed with pumice and water or oil .

Sanding sealer: see Sealer.

Sapstreak, pitch pockets: most often found in wood from coniferous trees. See Chapter 8.

Sealer: first coat on bare wood; often this is just shellac thinned at least 50 percent with denatured alcohol. This equalizes absorption of the stain which will follow.

Set: initial hardening of a finishing material. That is, when the liquid is dust-free but not yet completely hardened.

Shellac: lac suspended in an alcohol vehicle. Available in orange (natural) and bleached (white).

Size: see Sealer.

Softwood: woods from coniferous trees. (e.g., evergreens)

Solvent: any liquid that dissolves another material is the solvent for that material.

Stain: a transparent finishing material used to change the natural color of wood.

Tack cloth: fabric impregnated with varnish, oil, and water that remains sticky or tacky. Used to clean dust particles off a piece prior to staining or finishing. Also called tack rag.

Thinner: any material (e.g., solvent) used to thin the viscosity of another material.

Tipping off: using the dry tips of a bristle brush to lift off excess finish material to ensure a smooth, sagfree finish. This technique is used most often with varnishes and enamels.

Tung oil: drying oil made form the nuts of the Tung tree. Also called Chinawood oil.

Turpentine: volatile, colorless solvent distilled from pine tree secretions.

Urethane resin: synthetic resin formed by combining vegetable oils with certain uric acids.

Varnish: a resinous-based transparent finishing maerial. Dries by oxidation of its vehicle.

Varnish stain: varnish with stain mixed in. Use only when no other finishing method can be put to use: E.G., to hide an ugly wood or finish.

Vehicle: the liquid portion of a finishing material; made up of the binder, non-volatile and volatile thinners, but no pigment.

Volatile liquid: one which evaporates quickly at room temperature and atmospheric pressure.

Water stain: soluble dye in water.

Wood alcohol (methyl alcohol): alcohol distilled from wood.

APPENDIX

Products and information listed in this Appendix , to the best of my knowledge, are of a quality that will satisfy the user. All listings shown have either been reviewed or tested by the author; many of the products are personal favorites with which I have had great finishing and refinishing success. All items are intended to help the reader; if you cannot find a certain product locally, write the manufacturer to locate the nearest source in your area.

Inclusion of a product in this Appendix does not necessarily imply endorsement either by the Author or **Hammermark Associates**. Names and addresses are listed solely to serve as a convenience to readers.

ABRASIVES
Merit Abrasive Products, Inc., 201 W. Manville Street, Compton, CA 90224. *Sand-O-Flex, Grind-O-Flex.*

Quiksand, Zynolyte Products Co., 15700 S. Avalon Blvd., Compton, CA 90224. *Washable sanding blocks.*

ADHESIVES
Borden Home and Professional Products , Dept. HA, 180 E Broad St., Columbus, OH 43125. *Elmer's Glue-All, and Elmer's Professional Carpenter's Wood Glue.*

Loctite Corporation, Automotive & Consumer Group, 4450 Cranwood Court, Dept. HA, Cleveland, OH 44128. *A wide variety of adhesives, sealers, epoxies.*

Franklin Glue Company, Dept. HA, 2020 Bruck St., Columbus, OH 43207. *Hide glue, white glue, aliphatic resin glue.*

ASSOCIATIONS
American Plywood Association, Dept. HA, Box 11700, Tacoma, WA 98411. *Write for information on plywood and project ideas.*

National Paint and Coatings Association, 1500 Rhode Island Ave. NW, Washington DC 20005. *For information on all paints and finishes; some literature available.*

Western Wood Products Association (WWPA), Dept. HA, Yeon Building, 522 SW Fifth Ave., Portland, OR 97204-2122. *For information on soft woods, literature, idea books and DIY plan sheets.*

Wood Moulding and Millwork Producers Association (WMMPA), Box 25278, Portland OR 97225. *Moldings and trim information.*

BRONZING POWDER
United States Bronze Powders, Inc. Box 31, Rt. 202, Flemington, NJ 08822. *Available at well-stocked hobby and artist's supplies stores, and at some hardware and paint stores.*

CLEAR FINISHES
McCloskey Varnish Co., Dept. HA, 7600 State Rd., Philadelphia, PA 19136. *Varnishes in all finishes from dull to high gloss.*

Pratt & Lambert, Box 22, Dept. HA, Buffalo, NY 14240. *Varnishes in all finishes from dull to high gloss.*

Thompson & Formby Inc., Box 667, Dept. HA, Olive Branch, MS 38654; *brand name, Formby's Tung Oil Finish. Offers a complete line of refinishing and wood care products available at home centers and hardware stores nationwide. Write above address for catalog.*

Valspar Corporation, Specialties Division, Dept. HA, 1220 North Garnet Drive, North Lake, IL 60164. *Varnishes.*

ZAR, UGL, Dept. HA, Box 70, Scranton, PA 18501. *At paint and hardware stores; write maker for nearest dealer.*

CRAFTSMAN SUPPLY HOUSES

Albert Constantine & Son, Dept. HA, 2050 Eastchester Rd., Bronx, NY 10461.

The Woodworkers' Store, Dept. HA, 21801 Industrial Blvd., Rogers, MN 55374.

Woodcraft Supply, Dept. HA, 41 Atlantic Avenue, Box 4000, Woburn, MA 01888.

Note: All three craftsman houses listed above carry a full and complete line of tools and woodworker's products--including finishes.

DECOUPAGE

Home Products Division, Building 223-4S, Dept. HA, 3M Center, St. Paul, MN 55144. *Wet or dry sandpapers (very fine grit) intended for decoupage.*

FABRIC PROTECTION

3M Company, see address above. *Scotchgard.*

FURNITURE PLANS

Hammermark Associates, Dept. FB, Box 201, Floral Park, N. Y. 11002. *Authentic designs for Country Furniture; fully detailed plans. Send $1. for catalog; refunded with first order.*

HARDWARE

Amerock Corp., Dept. HA, 4000 Auburn St., Rockford, IL 61125-7018. *Distinctive, quality decorative hardware; also a complete line of magnetic and friction catches, hinges and drawer slides.*

W & L Manufacturing Co., Inc., Dept. HA, 343 Cortland St., Belleville, NJ 07109. *Leveltite fasteners.*

LIQUID SANDER

UGL, Dept. HA, Box 70, Scranton, PA. 18501. *At paint and hardware stores; write maker for nearest dealer.*

LITERATURE
(recommended reading)

A. Constantine & Son, Dept. HA, 2050 Eastchester Rd. Bronx, N.Y. 10461. *"Veneering Simplified", by Harry Hobbs*

Formica Corp., Dept. HA, 1 Stanford Road, Piscataway, NJ 08144. 1-800-524-0159 *"Do-It-Yourself with Formica".*

National Paint & Coatings Assn., 1500 Rhode Island Ave. NW, Dept. HA, Wash., DC 20005. *"Proper Care of Furniture Finishes".*

Rohm and Haas Co., Advertising Dept., (HA), Independence Mall West, Phila., PA 19105. *Send for Plexiglas literature, including their how-to booklet.*

PAINT, AUTHENTIC COUNTRY

The Stulb Paint & Chemical Company, Dept. HA, 618 West Washington Street, Norristown, PA 19404. 1-800-221-8444. *Old Village and Sturbridge paint colors.*

PAINT, MILK

The Old Fashioned Milk Paint Co., Dept. HA, Box 222-HA, Groton, MA 01450.

Stulb Paint & Chemical Co. *See address above.*

PAINT, SPRAY

Borden Chemical, Dept. HA, 180 E. Broad St., Columbus, OH 43215. *Krylon--at paint, hardware and crafts supplies stores.*

PAINT & VARNISH REMOVER

Thompson & Formby Inc., Box 667, Dept. HA, Olive Branch, MS 38654. *Formby's Paint Remover, also available in aerosol.*

PAINTBRUSH CLEANER

Savogran, Dept. HA, Box 130, Norwood, Mass. 02062. *At paint and hardware stores.*

PAINTING/REFINISHING TIPS & INFORMATION

Sears, Roebuck & Co. *For answers to questions about painting and paint products, call: 1-800-9-PAINTS, Mon. through Sat.; 9AM to 5PM, Central Time.*

Thompson & Formby Inc., Box 667, Olive Branch, MS 38654. *For answers to questions about refinishing, staining, applying finishes, wood care and maintenance, repairing minor injuries and more. Send details/questions to above address.*

PASTE WOOD FILLER

Benjamin Moore & Co., Dept. HA, Chestnut Ridge Rd., Montvale, N.J. 07645. *Trade name, Benwood; available where B. Moore products are sold.*

PLASTICS

Formica Corp., Dept. HA, 1 Stanford Road, Piscataway, NJ 08144. 1-800-524-0159. *High pressure plastic laminates, contact cement.*

Kampel Enterprises, Inc., Dept. HA, Dillsburg, PA 17019. *Seamfil, a filler for laminate surfaces.*

Rohm & Haas Co., Advertising Dept. (HA), Independence Mall West, Phila., PA. 19105. *Send for Plexiglas literature.*

WilsonArt, Ralph Wilson Plastics Co., Dept. HA, Temple, TX 76501.

PROFESSIONAL STRIPPING

BIX Process Systems Inc., Dept. HA, 6 Clarke Circle, P.O. Box 309, Bethel, CT 06801. *Write for information on franchises, systems, products and methods.*

REFINISHERS

Thomas & Formby Inc., Dept. HA, Box 667, Olive Branch, MS. 38654; *brand name, Formby's Furniture Refinisher. Offers a complete line of refinishing and wood care products available at home centers and hardware stores nationwide. Write above address for catalog.*

Minwax Co. Inc. Dept. HA, 102 Chestnut Ridge Plaza, Montvale, NJ 07645.

UGL, Dept. HA, Box 70, Scranton, PA 18501.

STAINS

Beverlee's Wood Finishing Products, UGL, Dept. HA, Box 70, Scranton, PA 18501.

Minwax Co. See *Refinishers* for address.

PPG Industries, 1 PPG Place 13 South, Dept. HA, Pittsburgh, PA 15272.

Thompson & Formby, Inc., Box 667, Dept. HA, Olive Branch, MS 38654. *Homer Formby's Jelled Wiping Stains.*

ZAR Wood Finishing Products, UGL, Dept. HA, Box 70, Scranton, PA 18501.

STENCIL SUPPLIES

Adele Bishop, Inc., Box 557-HA, Manchester, VT 05254. *A full line of stenciller's supplies.*

TACK CLOTHS

Louis M. Gerson Co., Inc., Dept. HA, Middleboro, MA 02346. *At well-stocked paint and hardware stores.*

TOOLS

Adjustable Clamp Co., Dept. HA, 417 No. Ashland Ave., Chi., IL 60622. *Full line of quality clamps; at hardware stores and building supplies centers.*

Black & Decker Mfg. Co., Dept. HA, 10 North Park Drive, Hunt Valley, MD. 21030. *Portable power tools.*

Delta International, Dept. HA, 246 Alpha Drive, Pitts., PA 15238. *Excellent line of stationary power tools.*

Dremel Mfg. Co., 4915 21st St. Dept. HA, Racine, Wi. 53406. *Pioneering firm in small shop tools including Moto-Tool, Mini-Lathe, Moto-Shop Scroll Saw/Sander, Disc Belt Sander, 4"-dia. Blade Bench Saw.*

Hyde Mfg. Co., 54 Eastford Rd., Dept. HA, Southbridge, Mass. 01550. *Tools for painters and finishers.*

Makita USA Inc., Dept. HA., 12950 E. Alondra Blvd., Cerritos, CA 90701-2194. *Portable power tools.*

Porter-Cable Corp., Dept. HA, Young's Crossing at Hwy. 45, Box 2468, Jackson, TN. 38302-2468. *Portable power tools.*

Red Devil Inc., 2400 Vauxhall Rd., Union, N.J. 07083. *Tools for painters and finishers.*

Ryobi America Corp., Dept. HA, 1158 Tower Lane, Bensenville, IL. 60106. *Portable power tools.*

Skil Corp., Dept. HA, 4801 W. Peterson Ave., Chicago, IL. 60646. *Portable power tools.*

Stanley Tools, Dept. HA, Box 1800, Advertising Services, New Britain, CT 06050. *Hand tools.*

WAX

The Butcher Polish Co., Dept. HA, 120 Bartlett Street, Marlborough, MA 01752-3013. *Butcher's WHITE DIAMOND Bowling Alley Paste Wax (clear) and Butcher's BOSTON POLISH Paste Was (amber tinted) for fine furniture.*

Hammermark Associates, Dept. FB, P.O. Box 201, Floral Park, N.Y. 11002. *The craftsman's favorite----BRIWAX; available in natural and tinted versions. Excellent furniture wax. Write for price information.*

INDEX